Praise for the author

Whether in her talks or writings, Raheel Raza has always engaged humanity in a moral discourse where all human beings can connect with each other based on common ethical values. In this work, she has courageously sought to incorporate notions of dignity, freedom of conscience, rights of minorities, and gender equality based on the notion of universal moral values. In the process, she engages and challenges the juridical and exegetical formulations of the classical period of Islam.

- *Dr. Liyakatali Takim, University of Denver*

If it were possible to achieve peace and harmony throughout the world through the efforts of one person, that person would be Raheel Raza. There is no one more passionate and more committed to the cause. When she speaks, people listen.

- *Carola Vyhnak, Manager of Community and Public Relations, The Toronto Star*

Raheel Raza is one of the most highly respected scholars in the field of Inter-faith studies that I have the privilege to know. On several occasions, we have worked together on presentations designed to facilitate relationships between the Muslim and Christian communities. She is a very able communicator, and very dialogical in her educational approach. Her analytical insights are sharp, and extremely valued by the wider community. That is part of the reason her frequent articles in The Toronto Star are so well received. There are few scholars I know who have a greater grasp of the current inter-faith issues that challenge us, and who are able to make the connections between these issues and the political, economic and social contexts of our time. As a feminist scholar, she brings a fresh and often prophetic perspective to the raging religious and political debates in our world, and has the courage of her convictions in the process. She does this with the passion of commitment to her own religious tradition, and with deep respect for other paths of religious search and truth. Raheel Raza is dedicated to the pursuit of truth that frees and builds relationships among peoples of diverse cultures. Her scholarship is a reference point for many of us who seek a similar goal.

- *Dr. Hallett Llewellyn, Pastoral Staff, Trinity St. Paul's United Church, Toronto*

PREFACE

It has been my privilege to share a podium with Raheel Raza a number of times, and I find her to be a refreshingly moderate, progressive activist. Now, what do those words mean? As a responsible journalist, in these stories Raza illuminates us about the real meanings of these and many other terms, and helps educate us as we try to understand today's struggle within Islam, especially about the role of women and relations with the rest of the world. These highly readable essays open our eyes to the historical facts, and to both sides of many of the contentious issues. At times she even defends some traditional views.

At the same time she has a clear stance. One of my spiritual teachers once said, "Religion is progressive, if it's not progressive, it isn't religion." It is mainly in the last century that Judaism, the tradition I was born into, developed not only *conservative* and *reform* wings in addition to its *orthodox* heritage, but also *reconstructionist* and *renewal*. This happened in other faith groups, too; why not in Islam? While embracing her religion with renewed vigour, Raza is among those who insist on a renewed examination of the meanings of their faith, and in untangling the social and political burdens placed upon it over the centuries. And she gives us refreshing insights into the inner struggles that many are undergoing, in the greater *jihad* the Prophet spoke about.

She expresses special admiration for the Sufi mystics with their all-encompassing spirituality, and today's interfaith movement, with both of which I have the good fortune to be involved. She quotes the thirteenth century Sufi Master, Jalaluddin Rumi, who began as a pre-eminent Islamic scholar, and became one of the early interfaith spokesmen. Translations of his works are the most quoted poetry in the English language today. She also tells the entrancing story of the first Sufi Saint of Islam: Rabia, a woman!

Above all, this is not a scholarly tome full of footnotes, but an entertaining series of stories of interesting people, in the best tradition of the "new journalism", with the passionate engagement of the writer. It is fitting that among the many honours she has received was a tribute by *Canadian Living* magazine, for she perfectly exemplifies the progressive yet moderate stance that Canada is becoming respected for around the world.

-*Rev. Leslie Gabriel Mezei, interfaith minister of the Universal Worship Service and Editor of the Interfaith Unity e-mail newsletter (www.interfaithunity.ca)*

THEIR JIHAD...
NOT MY JIHAD!

To Tom

Peace

Raheel Raza

Raheel Raza

A Muslim Canadian woman speaks out

THEIR JIHAD...
NOT MY JIHAD!

 Basileia Books

Their Jihad...Not My Jihad! Copyright © 2005 by Raheel Raza. All rights reserved. Printed in Canada. No part of this book may be used or reproduced in any manner whatsoever without written permission except in case of brief quotations embodied in critical articles and reviews. For information address Basileia Books, 354476 Mill Line, Ingersoll, ON N5C 3J5.

National Library of Canada Cataloguing in Publication

Raza, Raheel, 1950-
Their Jihad...Not My Jihad! A Muslim Canadian woman speaks out / Raheel Raza

Includes bibliographical references.
ISBN 0-9735087-2-8

   1. Jihad. 2. Islam-21st century. 3. Muslim women. 4. Women in Islam.
1. Title.

BP 182.R39 2005   297.7'2   C2005-906250-9

Design & Composition: *Basileia Books*
Cover design: *Manuel Oliveira*
Cover photo: *CP (Hussein Malla)*
Back cover photo: *Karen Paton-Evans*
Editors: *Karen Paton-Evans and David Galston*
Printed in Canada by *Webcom*

DEDICATION

I dedicate this book
to the activists who are struggling to take back the soul of Islam
&
to the women of Islam who are struggling to bring about a "silent revolution"
&
to my friends in spirituality, who are struggling
to bridge the gulf between various faiths

ACKNOWLEDGEMENTS

This work would not have been possible without the support and guidance of my many mentors. I would like to especially thank Dr. Abdulaziz Sachedina, Professor of Islamic Studies, University of Virginia and of the International Advisory Board for the constitution of Iraq; The Rev. Dr. Karen Hamilton, General Secretary, The Canadian Council of Churches; and Dr. Liyakatali Takim, Professor of Religious Studies, University of Denver.

※

On a personal level, I am profoundly thankful to my husband, Sohail, who has been the inspiration for many of my writings, and for his complete confidence in me; I am touched by the unconditional love and unwavering support of my sons, Saif and Zain, and I am grateful to my mother-in-law, Nikhat, for her patience and forbearance.

※

I fondly remember my parents: Ammi for constantly admonishing me to "speak less" because girls should be seen and not heard and Abbajani for encouraging me to follow my dreams and reach for the stars. May their souls rest in peace. Ameen

※

I would like to acknowledge that many of these articles were initially published in The Toronto Star; I am grateful to the various editors who felt the message needed to be heard.

※

I thank the following organizations for their support:

Creative Cultural Communications
Forum for Learning
Muslim Canadian Congress
Organization of Islamic Learning
SnowStar Institute of Religion
The United Church of Canada
Women Engaging in Bridge Building

※

CONTENTS

Foreword, xiii
Introduction, xv

Part 1. Political Jihad - A Struggle for the Soul of Islam
1. Understanding jihad, 18
2. Oh Oklahoma - when will the violence against civilians stop?, 20
3. I came, I saw, I wept - a visit to the homeland, 23
4. An open letter to Osama bin Laden, 25
5. Faith of Love versus a Culture of Hate, 27
6. Muslims need tolerance and sacrifice, not suicide, 30
7. Pakistan, a country in denial, 34
8. Thoughts on the destruction of my homeland, 37
9. Their jihad is not my jihad, 38
10. Role of media in establishing peace in society, 41
11. Jihad in the newsroom, 45
12. Are our civil liberties at stake?, 50
13. Loyalty towards our adopted land, 54
14. Reality check on security checks, 56
15. A call to arms for moderate Muslims, 59
16. Three weddings and a funeral, 62
17. What led to the London bombings?, 64

Part 2. Gender Jihad - A Struggle for Women's Rights
1. The Silent Revolution - women in Islam, 68
2. To change the image of Muslims, let's begin with the women, 76
3. Silent shame: domestic violence crosses all cultural and ethnic boundaries, 78
4. Once again, 81
5. Memories are not enough, 82
6. Matchmaker in the South Asian community, 88
7. Covering my head does not make me brain-damaged!, 93
8. Lifting the veil of ignorance - Muslim women on religion, identity and way of life, 95
9. Death without honour, 98
10. Muslim scholar calls for reforms - women's rights, 102
11. Weaving a web of peace, 106
12. Weapons of mass instruction, 108

13. Justice is gender equality, 111
14. I am Woman, 115
15. From the ritual to the spiritual, 118

Part 3. Spiritual Jihad - A Struggle to Know Each Other
1. The need for compassion and tolerance, 124
2. Jesus in Islam, 127
3. The Whirling Dervishes in Toronto, 129
4. Pursuing peace through education and knowledge, 131
5. Building religious inclusivity in Ontario, 135
6. Reducing God to a policeman, 140
7. Order a Fatwa - delivered in 30 minutes or it's free!, 143
8. Do Muslims eat ketchup? Diversity in Islam, 146
9. American-Muslim convert critiques mosque culture, 154
10. The wisdom of listening - the power of commitment, 156
11. Beyond the fluff stuff, 161
12. Merry Christmas from a Merry Muslim, 164
13. Shari'a - it's about religious freedom, 166
14. Eid and awe in New York, 169
15. Peace, 173

Glossary, clxxiv
References, clxxv

FOREWORD

Jihad is probably one of the most misunderstood words in the world today by both Muslims and non-Muslims alike. The word means to strive, and it defines the Muslim "struggle" to do the will of Allah. This struggle is primarily a personal one but secondarily a social one. In both cases, since the struggle is to fulfill the will of a merciful and compassionate God, *jihad* involves putting aside personal and national ambitions for the betterment of humanity. That act at the very least is a fundamental part of compassion.

In *Their Jihad...Not My Jihad!* Raheel Raza takes on a "*jihad*" of her own. But hers is *jihad* in the traditional Islamic sense. Her interest is to "struggle" with the truth in an effort to find a faithful expression of Islam in the modern world. The tenets in her *jihad* are Islamic cornerstones: compassion, honesty and peace.

What is astounding is that only on rare occasions do our media giants and journalistic reporters manage to get it right. On a large scale, western society now by default knows *jihad* only through hatred, destruction and suicide bombers. An honourable word in the Islamic tradition has become practically useless among Muslims who know its real meaning. The choice is either to reclaim the word or divorce oneself from its use.

Raheel Raza will not settle for a divorce. *Their Jihad...Not My Jihad!* seeks not only to reclaim the word but also the work of *jihad*. Raza sets on the table the heritage of Islam founded on the concern for justice, ripened by the fires of compassion, and expressed honestly in the skills of a critical thinker.

It would be right to say that this book of struggle concerns the struggle for the heart of Islam. Written in a journalistic style, the author offers analysis accessible to almost any reader, yet maintains an integrity of learnedness. For non-Muslims and quite possibly (and perhaps even mainly) for Muslims, there is sufficient commentary on the Qu'ran, the *Shari'a* and *Hadith* to make this a book of new insight. But what Raza involves the most is the outstanding Islamic tradition of Kalam or inquiry. This book is mainly an inquiry into issues that define our times and that challenge Islam as much as any other religion or ethical system. Indeed, we have here a journalistic *tour de force*.

Their Jihad...Not My Jihad! takes us through many moments of terror, of loss and of human tragedy. It brings us face to face with Western colonial history but does not ask us to excuse Islamic extremism by finding the scapegoat here. It raises issues that non-Muslims probably wonder about but politely never ask. And it offers several moving essays on feminism in Islam, which possibly constitutes the most significant location of *jihad*, that is, of justice making, among Muslims today.

But its main point may well be that it sets out to correct a growing misconception and misrepresentation not only of Muslims internationally but our world as a whole. A journalist herself, Raza places the blame fairly openly at the feet of the media. In this book, she breaks through what she calls a "jingoism" of journalism that focuses on sensationalism and virtually ignores the task of exposing the truth. "Thousands of innocent civilians are dying everyday in other parts of the world and receive little or no recognition by media. Second, there were [before and after September 11] many peace-making and bridge building stories that have never been told." Raza asks why Jerry Falwell's claim that the Prophet Mohammad was a terrorist should earn a featured place on 60 *Minutes* but such important initiatives like Woman Engaged in Bridge Building (WEBB), an organization of action and of hope, remain virtually unknown.

What this book does in a most significant way is tell the untold story. It relays a point of view of a woman with vast experience. She awakens us to the world of Islam that few Westerners know and that certainly the media will not cover. We become acquainted with many Muslim personalities who work for peace and justice, who are motivated by hearts of compassion, who receive rare public acknowledgement, and who carry out a silent *jihad* for an Islam of faithful expression. This is Islam in the way the West does not know it, publicly, but that is in fact Islam in its true colours: a religion of beauty, of artistic achievement, and above all, of love for others.

Raheel Raza is known to me through Canada's SnowStar Institute of Religion. It is my honour to write the forward for this book that represents her great passion. It is also my privilege to recommend this book to the widest possible audience. Open your hearts. Let religion in our world be defined by an openness of mind and an honesty of soul. Raza reminds us that these qualities are Islamic to the core and that the struggle to reclaim them is a *jihad* of great nobility.

- *Rev. Dr. David Galston, President, SnowStar Institute of Religion and Fellow of the Jesus Seminar*

INTRODUCTION

Bismillah, Ar-Rahman Ar-Raheem
In the name of God, the Beneficent, the Merciful

This book is a compilation of my feelings and ideas, starting long before 9/11, when I left my country of birth, Pakistan, with deep emotions and a heavy heart.

I saw the Islam that I love and venerate was being hijacked with the introduction of a new fundamentalism and the rise of the Taliban. I was deeply troubled by the treatment of half of the Muslim population – women whose voices were rarely heard over babble of extremist voices.

I was considered a rebel because I spoke out against injustice. In 1988, I came to Canada with my husband and two sons. Here I broadened my Islamic horizons and learned to strengthen my spirituality by interacting with people of various traditions.

Subsequently, world events spiralled out of control into chaos and we saw the madness of 9/11 followed by the so-called war on terror: the invasion of Afghanistan and Iraq. I found I had a different kind of challenge on my hands – a challenge to separate culture from religion; truth and justice from propaganda, and the ritual from the spiritual.

A lot has been said and written about the political causes that led to the rise of terrorism. This started with the involvement of the CIA in ousting the Russians from Afghanistan, and most of all, the inability of the West to deal with the geo-political situation arising in the Muslim world, especially the plight of the Palestinian people.

I am shattered when my faith is blamed for the current crisis facing humanity.

This book comprises articles, speeches, poems and interviews of religious scholars and activists. Some were written prior to September 11, 2001 in an effort to educate people about Islam. Looking at the dates these articles were originally written, some seem prophetic, in light of the events that followed.

Similar but more impassioned writings and interviews after 9/11 became a quest to undertake "damage control" and to critique the ideology that has permeated my faith and continues to influence thousands of fellow Muslims.

These writings also address the movement by Muslim women, which I call "The Silent Revolution".

All this comes from the heart.

Raheel Raza, Toronto, September 11, 2005

PART 1

POLITICAL JIHAD -
A STRUGGLE FOR THE SOUL OF ISLAM

"Killing one person is as though he killed all of humanity"
The Qur'an

⊱⊰

UNDERSTANDING JIHAD

There are five pillars of faith in Islam, which include belief in one God, fasting, prayer, going for the pilgrimage and giving charity. Some religious authorities claim a sixth pillar: *Jihad*. In the past decade, this word has become well known in English because of the contemporary world situation which has made it the focus of media, which have very often used it out of context.

Interpreting the term *jihad* to mean "holy war" is misleading and usually inaccurate. The Qur'anic usage of the term *jihad* is much broader than the political use of term might imply. The basic meaning of *jihad* is "struggle" and this struggle is not necessarily an armed struggle. It can mean the struggle for truth and justice or good over evil.

When we understand the word Islam to mean "submission" or "surrender", then in a certain manner, *jihad* complements Islam. This surrender is not passive behaviour, but takes place actively and willingly to God's command, since it is for God's will that people struggle in his path. Hence, submission demands struggle. In order to submit fully to God's commands, people need to be aware of all that is evil or negative around them and within themselves that pulls them away from God. Therefore, submission to God and struggle in his path go together hand-in-hand, and neither is complete without the other.

Within the Islamic context, the fact that submission to God demands struggle in his path is self-evident. The basic tenets of Islam, fasting, prayer and pilgrimage are all achieved through inner struggle. It takes a great deal of self control and struggle to submit to an unseen higher authority and also to deal with the pressure of society to conform.

The true meaning and place of *jihad* in a Muslim's life is illustrated through a well-known tradition of the Prophet Mohammad. When he had returned to Medina from a battle with the enemies of the new religion, he is quoted to have said, "We have returned from the lesser *jihad* to the greater *jihad*." The people asked, "O Messenger of God, what *jihad* could be greater than struggling against the unbelievers?" He replied, "Struggling against the enemy in your own breast."

Muslim scholars who claim that *jihad* is a sixth pillar of Islam usually refer to the fact that struggle in the path of God is a necessity for all Muslims. It is also recognized that this struggle will sometimes take the role of outward war against the enemies of Islam. The Qur'an also says that in some cases war becomes a contingency – especially as a means of self-defence. In chapter two of the Qur'an, it says: "war may become necessary only to stop evil from triumphing in a way that would corrupt the earth."

It needs to be stressed that war is only acceptable as a means of self-defence and to protect the faith. In times of war, stringent rules are applicable. The Qur'an says: "and slay not the life which Allah has made sacred, save in the course of justice." The Prophet of Islam told his companions and followers in the instance of the first war of Islam, when their lives were threatened and they had to revert to self-defence, that they could never harm innocent people, children, civilians, old people, people engaged in any worship or destroy crops and animals. The Qur'an says clearly: "only the combatants are to be fought and no more harm should be caused to them than they have caused." Thus wars and weapons of destruction that destroy civilians and their towns are totally ruled out by the Qur'an and by practice of the Prophet.

In current times, there is a huge debate taking place about the way terrorists interpret the Qur'an to justify *jihad* to mean violence. Karen Armstrong, in an article for The Guardian, entitled "Unholy Understanding of Holy Texts", writes that we distort our scriptures if we read them in an exclusively literal sense. She explains that all verses in the Qur'an are called "parables" (*ayat*) and its images of paradise, hell and the last judgment are also *ayat* - pointers to transcendent realities that we can only glimpse through signs and symbols. Armstrong clarifies that this is the reason Muslim extremists have given the *jihad* (which they interpret as "holy war") a centrality that it never had before and have thus redefined the meaning of Islam for many Muslims. She also says that in this they are often unwillingly aided by media, who also concentrate obsessively on the more aggressive verses of the Qur'an, without fully appreciating how these are qualified by the text as a whole.

OH OKLAHOMA – WHEN WILL THE VIOLENCE AGAINST CIVILIANS STOP?
May 1995

As a mother I am shattered and my heart weeps for the parents of the children killed in Oklahoma. As a human being I am horrified and appalled about the tragic events in a peaceful city that is forced to focus on the ongoing discovery of dead bodies amidst the debris that was once an inhabited building.

I cannot begin to comprehend or accept that there are people living in the civilized world who will stoop to violent and barbaric attacks on innocent men, women and children. Right now, I ache for those who have lost family and friends in the bombing. If I hurt thousands of miles away, I wonder how the residents of Oklahoma feel. I don't think I can even begin to gauge the depth of their despair and grief.

For whatever its worth, I do share in their anguish. If the survivors of this recent and uncalled for hideous attack on civilians feel malice and outrage at the offenders, they have every right to do so. I also abhor and despise the attackers for their cowardly act as I'm sure millions of other people do.

Because acts of brutality against innocent human beings can never be justified.

Media and politicians are looking for suspects, reasons and motives. They have called out their experts in terrorism, in Middle East politics and criminologists. I feel, however, there is no reasoning behind terrorism. There is never a motive behind killing innocent people except a depraved mind. If they do find who executed the bombing and why they did it, will it lessen the agony of those affected? Of course I understand that an investigation has to be made, but in the meantime we cannot just stand by waiting for something to happen. We must extend our compassion and our heartfelt sympathy to those touched by this gruesome tragedy.

It might help the people of Oklahoma and those around them to understand that most people, regardless of nationality, faith, culture or creed are with them in their time of crisis. We do not defend the motive or the criminals. Whether it is gas poisoning in Japan, suicide in Waco Texas, a bombing at the Trade Centre in New York or a pipe blast in Charlottetown, we are equally distressed by the incident. There is absolutely no place in civilized society for blatant acts of terrorism and we as nations, communities and also as individuals *must* openly condemn these acts and ensure ways to eradicate the diabolic evil that has infiltrated our society.

It has become the norm to tie in acts of terrorism with religious groups. Tell me which religion advocates killing of innocent people? Certainly not any faith with which I am familiar. And if there are people out there who commit ghastly crimes in the name of religion, then they need to be ousted from that religion because they are maligning the faith of others and putting it to test.

There is no excuse or provocation in any religion that condones senseless killing. In fact, most major religions of the world condemn senseless acts of violence and are trying to propagate peace in the world.

Those who do not adhere to policies of peace, love and goodwill towards all are obviously from a cult or fanatic organization that does not draw its mandate or strength from a religion. There is no place for such radicals in the pursuit of any faith and to accept such maniacs is to lead to eventual eradication of human values that we hold dear to us. Many of us came to North America to escape the influence of extremists who massacre, mutilate and destroy in the name of religion. Unfortunately, today religion is used as a crutch for many inhuman acts of depravity and this trend must be stopped.

If we are to live in a peace-loving society, then we must unanimously condemn terrorism and acts of brutality no matter who masterminds them. It is our right as free human beings and our responsibility to those around us to ensure the world remains free of slaughter and destruction.

I realize that America at one time or the other has meddled in affairs of many countries resulting in bloodshed and the loss of millions of lives. Saddam Hussein living free today is an example of the terror America has unleashed on the Middle East. Saddam alone is responsible for the destruction of millions of innocent men, women and children. Today, the killing fields of Russia, Bosnia and Rwanda are marked with the blood of the innocent. However, that still does not justify the senseless bombing in Oklahoma. Violence cannot be fought with counter violence. It just makes the circle a never ending round of dead bodies - which does not achieve anything in the end.

Right now people in Oklahoma, Charlottetown and New York are living in fear of what will happen next and glancing at each other in suspicion. This is the legacy of terrorism and we want no part in it. We as human beings are saddened, devastated and shocked by all incidents of violence.

Let us take a united stand and unanimously condemn all acts of terror in the past and the present and struggle together to create a peaceful future for our children.

I CAME, I SAW, I WEPT - A VISIT TO THE HOMELAND
June 2001

I CAME:

- because Karachi was once my City of Joy
- because I had not visited for many years due to the turmoil and unrest
- because my brother was taken into custody in an extrajudicial arrest
- because I naively thought there is still some semblance of sanity left and there would be justice
- because I had forgotten that in the jungle, only might prevails over right
- because my family is still here, so a part of my heart is still here to rejuvenate my spirit and revitalise my soul, through interaction with my loved ones, through those buried here and those still living
- because the smells and sounds of this ghost city still haunt me
- I came because I truly wanted to believe that all the horror stories I heard about my land of birth are not true

I SAW (Not with my eyes but with my heart and mind)

- the raw and wounded soul of this battered city
- violence and victimization; torture and treachery; corruption and cruelty; havoc and heartache
- more exposed guns and ammunition than I thought imaginable
- that there are no more Pakistanis left - only Sindhis, Punjabis, Pathans and Baluchis
- that there are no more Muslims left - only Shias, Sunnis, Ahmedis, Wahabis and the "Holier-than-Thou"
- that every person has a price
- a brazen show of unlimited wealth
- heartrending poverty with hungry children on the street

- the rape and massacre of poor, innocent people, feeding the fear that infiltrates the masses
- I saw decadence at its height, embodied in:
    - far-out, freaky and funky fashion shows
    - weddings lasting shamelessly for four weeks
    - bragging begums in beauty parlours and clubs competing for clients at every corner
    - cheap thrills on cellular phones
    - proud politicians in Porches guarded by gun-toting lunatics
    - Pashminas and passion as part of the social scene
    - a mindless generation of MTV, PTV and ZTV kids
    - families shattered by events they have no control over
- I saw a nation without a conscience and without a voice

I WEPT:

- for the people who cannot speak because they are victimized
- for those who can speak but will not raise their voices
- for the women who are treated as if they have no minds nor souls
- for those who have sold their souls and their consciences
- for those who have no choices
- for the cause of martyrs on whose blood this country was built
- for the dream of Allama Iqbal and Mohammad Ali Jinnah, the founding fathers of this country
- most of all I wept for myself because the country I once called home – Pakistan, land of the Pure, is no more.

AN OPEN LETTER TO OSAMA BIN LADEN: FROM A MUSLIM WOMAN WHO REFUSES TO BE TERRORISED
September 2001

Mr. bin Laden:

Although you have no authority nor standing in my eyes to call an entire community to *jihad*, still I am taking up your call. *Jihad* is the "struggle of good over evil". Therefore, my *jihad* is to expose you and people like you, and to prove that you derive your convoluted knowledge of Islam and the Qur'an from sources known only to yourself. The *jihad* that you call "Holy war" is not mentioned anywhere in the Qur'an. However, I will draw your attention to the verse in which the merciful and compassionate creator of the Universe, Allah, has likened the killing of one person as "though he killed all of mankind".

You, Mr. bin Laden, are an evil person and the war you are waging now is neither holy nor justified. Nor were the acts of hijacking and terrorism anything else but wrong. According to Islam, an attack against innocent people is cowardice and an expression of rejection of God's blessings. That is, of course, the God that we believe in: the God of mercy and love.

Since you call yourself a Muslim and continue to use the name of God to invoke your horrific message, you must be aware that the Qur'an has an entire chapter devoted to the concept of "*munafiq*" (hypocrite). History tells us that even 1,400 years ago, in the time of Prophet Mohammad (peace be upon him), there were elements within Islam, people who called themselves Muslim but caused more harm to Islam than the disbelievers. It was to warn the Prophet of such factors that God sent the verse to beware of the hypocrites.

You, Mr. bin Laden, as a true example of the *Munifiqeen*, have taken Islam back 1,400 years. You are nothing but a hypocrite trying to rouse ignorant people to acts of violence in the name of the same God who says so clearly in Qur'an: "O people we have formed you into nations and tribes so that you may know one another."

Having said this, we also have something to thank you for. In your acts of senseless violence and madness, you have cleared the air for those

Muslims who were confused. What you have done is shown very clearly to the world that there are two Islams being practiced today – one, the Islam of Prophet Mohammad - the Islam of peace and love, of forgiveness and compassion, of tolerance and spirituality, women's rights and equality. The other Islam is the militant, extremist, fanatic cult of those who misappropriate religious teachings to justify murder, inflict destruction on human society in the name of *Shari'a*, subjugate and suppress minorities and women to promote injustice, and have a philosophy that fellow Muslims who don't subscribe to their brand of religiosity are heretics.

Having hijacked our faith, you have not only brought about the wrath of the people you call your enemy, but also the wrath of the true believers who believe in truth over lies, justice over injustice, bravery and chivalry over the cowardice of hurting innocent civilians, and the beauty of celebrating life as a blessing from God rather than ending it in a futile attempt to reach paradise.

Mr. bin Laden, you appear to give very compelling reasons for your actions. At the top of your list are your hatred of the West and its oppression of Muslim lands.

My questions for you are: Where were you when Saddam Hussein was torturing Muslims in Iraq? What have you done personally to alleviate the suffering of Iraqi children? Did you or your organization *al Qaeda* build any hospitals, supply medicines or promote education in third world countries? Did you lobby to find a peaceful solution to the Palestine problem? And, instead of hiding like a mole under the hills of Afghanistan, why aren't you fighting this inane battle from the land of your birth instead of compromising the lives of innocent Afghani civilians who are already terrorized by your supporters - the Taliban?

FAITH OF LOVE VERSUS A CULTURE OF HATE
November 2001

Among the many e-mails being forwarded on the Internet post-September 11, one struck a strong chord. This is from an American who asks, "Why should I be the target audience of what 'true' Islam is? I don't need to know....tell the Muslims who have their Qur'an and Sunnah all backwards.....I don't want to hear the history of the Crusades or U.S. foreign policy and the C.I.A.....why is there no overt and highly visible attempt to re-educate error-laden believers to the 'true' message of Islam and Prophet Mohammad? I'm confused."

She's not the only one. Some Muslims are confused, too - especially those who understand that it's no longer an issue of "blame-the-victim" or devious political conspiracies. The message is clear that many Muslims are not *practising* the faith the way it was taught by Mohammad - so we have to find a solution within Islam.

While some voices are heard, reproving the misuse of Islam, we have to go a few steps further and actually implement solutions. Those countries or individuals who acquiesce to acts of terror, or worst still, give tacit approval to violence or murderous acts in the name of God, have to be strongly criticized and condemned.

This is not an easy task when fanatics and extremists have already hijacked our faith and when moderate voices are not heard over the babble of hate-mongering. Granted, the Muslim majority is not prone to violence and fanaticism, but many of us are to blame for remaining quiet and allowing religious zealots to practise various forms of terrorism within Muslim societies without fear of punishment or retaliation.

For example, Pakistan, which is currently prominent as an ally, has harboured and promoted domestic terrorism for the past two decades. In Pakistan, anyone with a weapon has the freedom to kill another human being without fear of reprisal. There is no accountability, so no one gets caught, let alone punished. Sectarian violence, in which Muslims have killed Muslims of other sects in the name of God, has been rife. Fortunately, everyone who is sane agrees that Pakistan President Pervez Musharraf is now in a pivotal position to change the course of events in his country - both politically and religiously.

As a result of regulations like the Blasphemy Law, minorities like the Ahmeddiya have been persecuted. (The form for passport issuance and renewal in Pakistan needs the applicant to sign a statement to the effect that the Ahmeddiya community is not part of Islam.) The Christian community in Pakistan is one of the most peace-loving and passive communities that has lived in harmony with its fellow Pakistanis for many years. Sadly, the recent massacre of 18 Christian worshippers in Bahawalpur, Pakistan is only one example of ongoing genocide. Ironically, Pakistan was built on the foundation of Islam - the true face of Islam that grants freedom and protection to minorities.

So where did all this bigotry come from? Intolerance and persecution of minorities came about due to a culture of hate and violence, which was allowed to permeate places of worship. Instead of expressing the message of tolerance and love, which is essential to Islam, a convoluted message of hate and venom has been sent forth. Unfortunately, few speak out against these atrocities and if they do, they are quickly silenced.

What needs to be done? The solution, I believe, lies with the silent majority in Islam who need to speak up and ensure the hateful rhetoric and actions of people like Osama bin Laden and his supporters die before they takes root. They need to ensure the pulpit of a mosque is not used to spew hate, and most of all, they need to empower other Muslims to take action against injustice, intolerance and violence wherever it is happening.

Whether this is done through the law, state or a group of individuals, the acts of removing such criminals should be swift and supported by all Muslims if they want to ensure the sanctity of Islam the way it was taught by the Prophet. We must reiterate that Islam was and should remain a message of peace and love.

The few of us who do speak out will face resistance and criticism. But maybe what we need right now is a renaissance or revival in Islam to clean out the extremist elements that have muddied our clean image. For this to happen, we have to first accept that the enemy is not outside, but within us. Islam has a history of those who have harmed the faith from within. These people are called *"munafiq"* or hypocrites and a message was sent to the Prophet Mohammad, warning him against the *munafiq* who cause more harm to the faith than anyone from the outside could ever accomplish.

Osama bin Laden and those who propagate a culture of hate and violence are perfect examples of such hypocrites and need to be exposed, condemned and charged. This will not happen with weapons and missiles - it has to happen through political strength and the might of the Muslim world, which can wield a strong influence on those who have the capabilities to find and eradicate terrorism.

It is about time Muslims stopped living in denial, woke up and started publicly and privately taking action against those who blatantly and brazenly misuse our faith.

Simultaneously, Muslims have to empower foreign governments who support and finance countries like Pakistan to ensure the aid is contingent upon restoration of human rights and the eradication of domestic terrorism.

MUSLIMS NEED TOLERANCE AND SACRIFICE, NOT SUICIDE
March 2002: Advent of the Islamic New Year

"Infuse your heart with mercy, love and kindness for your subjects....either they are your brothers in religion or your equals in creation." Caliph Ali bin Abu Talib (d. 661)

The Islamic New Year (a lunar calendar ten days short of the Gregorian) is called *Moharram*. This is a time for deep reflection and retrospection for Muslims worldwide and tells of one of the most significant events of sacrifice in Muslim History. This is the sacrifice of Imam Hussain, grandson of the Prophet Mohammad, for good over evil. Throughout this month, stories are retold of the importance of sacrifice and tolerance, two essentials of Islam that many of us seem to have forsaken.

In the West, Islam is generally looked upon as a religion of force and violence and regarded as being very intolerant. It is unfortunate that incidents like the horrific massacre of Christians in an Islamabad mosque and the alarmingly frequent crimes of suicide bombers only fuel this image. Despite extremist criminal actions, Islam is essentially a faith of peace and tolerance.

In the Encyclopedia Americana, the meaning of tolerance is to bear, to endure, to put up with. In recent times, however, the meaning and range of the subject have changed. There is no equivalent term in the Arabic language to mean what is traditionally understood in English by tolerance. The word that is used in Arabic is *tasamuh*. The root form of this word has two connotations – generosity and ease. Thus, for Muslims, tolerance indicates generosity and ease from both sides on a reciprocal basis.

Tolerance is the cornerstone of Islam and has emerged out of the very nature and history of Islam. Being the youngest of the three monotheistic faiths, the Qur'anic revelation came at a time when Christians and Jews were already practicing their faith and living with the Muslims. Recognizing that Christians and Jews were faithful people, the Qur'an called them *ahl-al-kitaab* or people of the book (the book being the Torah or the Bible). Traditionally, Muslims did not view Christians and Jews as minorities in the way that other religions in the West are now described. The Qur'an, therefore, proactively discusses relationships with non-Muslims as well as giving direction as to how Muslims should treat others around them.

Through the Qur'an, God addresses all people and says: "*O mankind we created you from a single pair of a male and female and made you into nations and tribes so that you may know each other. Verily the most honoured of you in the sight of God is the most righteous of you, and God has full knowledge and is well acquainted with all things.*"

The diversity of races, colours and creeds in the world are seen as a sign of God's blessing and should lead to closeness rather than racism and intolerance. Therefore, tolerance has been a natural, inseparable part of Islam from the beginning. Muslims did not tolerate non-Muslims grudgingly, but welcomed them to live feely in Muslim society, giving them protection and not forcing them to fight their battles. At the height of Islam's success, the Qur'an set the principle of "*there is no compulsion religion*" as well as "*to me my religion, to you is yours.*"

The Qur'an affirms that God has created people to be different and that they will always remain different not only in their appearance but also in their beliefs. Unity of humans does not necessarily mean uniformity.

The Qur'an refers to the people of the book in a positive light. It says: "*They are not alike. Of the people of the book there is a staunch community who recite the revelations of God in the night season, falling prostrate before him. They believe in God and the last day and enjoin right conduct and forbid indecency and vie with one another in good works. These are of the righteous.*" Similarly, the Qur'an allows Muslims to eat the food of the people of the book and to marry their women.

Referring to the Prophets that came before Mohammad, the Qur'an says "*Muhammad is but a messenger, before whom other messengers were sent.*"

The Qur'an also guides Muslims to appeal to the people of book through what is common between them. The Qur'an says, "*O people of the book – come to common terms as between us and you: that we have to worship none but God, that we associate no partners with him, that we erect not from among ourselves Lords and patrons other than God.*"

In the Qur'an, God addresses Muslims and the followers of other religions, saying, "*We have ordained a law and assigned a path to each of you. Had God pleased he could have made you one nation, but it is his wish to prove you by that which he has bestowed upon you. Vie then with each other in good works, for to God you shall all be returned and he shall declare to you what you have disagreed about."*

This direction to leave differences to be settled on the Day of Judgment is repeated many times in the Qur'an. Even in their relations with polytheists, who stand as the extreme opposite of the Islamic belief in monotheism, Muslims are instructed in the Qur'an: *"God does not forbid you to be kind and equitable to those who do not fight for you or your faith and do not drive you out of your home for God loves those who are just."*

The Qur'an further instructs Muslims not to argue with the people of the book and to deal with them in a fair way. The Qur'an advises Muslims to say to the people of the book, *"We believe in what has been revealed to us, and in what has been revealed to you. Our Lord and your Lord is one and the same and to him we submit ourselves."*

When the Muslims of Arabia, under their ruler, Caliph Umar, entered Jerusalem (then called Aeilia) in 638 AD, Umar made the following agreement with the inhabitants, in accordance with Qur'anic injunctions:

"This is the security which Umar, the servant of God, the commander of the faithful, grants to the people of Aeilia. He grants to all, whether sick or sound, security for their lives, their possessions, their churches and their crosses, and for all that concerns their religion. Their churches shall not be changed into dwelling places, nor destroyed nor the crosses of the inhabitants, nor aught of their possessions, nor shall any constraint be put on them in matters of faith, nor shall any of them be harmed."

This was modeled on the life of the Prophet as he followed the command of God through the Qur'an. Muslims allowed non-Muslims to live in accordance to their customs even if these were forbidden in Islam. Thus Christians were allowed to breed pigs, eat pork and make and drink alcohol in Muslims countries, even though these are forbidden to Muslims.

Today, tolerance refers to tolerating people, beliefs and traditions that are different from one's own. While globalization enhances this cause, it is also heightened by the lack of religion in people's lives around the world. Sometimes tolerance in current terms refers to political correctness. However, the Islamic ideal is not to just accept, but to embrace those who are different without compromising one's own principles.

Islam ordains enjoining the good and forbidding what is wrong and does not allow practices that fundamentally undermine the family system. For example, it would not recommend campaigning for the decriminalization of drugs.

Muslims are under obligation not to force their religious norms on others; to live under the law of the land, provided it does not go against the principles of Islam.

PAKISTAN, A COUNTRY IN DENIAL
May 2002

Since my arrival to Canada in 1989, I have returned to visit Pakistan, my land of birth, at least once a year. My visits help me to stay in touch with my roots and also allow me to keep a keen eye on the political pulse of this volatile country.

As I traveled to Karachi a few weeks ago, I was a bit apprehensive because post-9/11, Pakistan has been in the eye of the storm. Pakistanis in North America, shaken to the core, have been galvanized into dialogue, discussion and forums. I was curious to learn how people in Pakistan were reacting.

The mood is strange and unnatural for a country on the brink of nuclear war, faced with a massive crisis within its own ranks and a raging war in the neighbourhood. One section of the community (mostly the educated elite) is totally in denial and talks vulgarly about designer outfits, jewellery and decadent parties. It was the wedding season and "Monsoon Wedding" is not even close to the kind of pomp and glamour everyone is competing with.

At one Pakistani wedding, close to 10 tons of fresh flowers were used for just one ceremony and then left to rot on the street. It is typical for wedding clothing to cost anywhere from $1,150 to $1,750 CDN per ensemble – and that is just for the guests! The bride's designer outfit can cost between $5,800 to $23,250 CDN.

The price tags are staggering, considering the average annual income in Pakistan is $490 CDN per year. Thirty-five percent of the population lives below the poverty line.

With this crowd, there's no chance of a conversation about the realities of life or grass roots issues like human rights.

As a guest in my sister's home, I felt a bit decadent, attended by two cooks, two maids, two chauffeurs and two gardeners! I mentioned this to my sister and she justified the need for double caretakers as she has two daughters-in-law living with her. I think the real reason is that young people in upper middle class homes can't carry a dish to the sink or (God forbid) clean bathrooms. The worst day of their lives is when servants don't turn up for work. The servant problem is a really issue high on the priority list.

I managed to hold my tongue and not rock the boat. After all, it's a great holiday when one is not involved in any physical or mental exercise. I was served tea in bed everyday; was offered a menu of choices for lunch, tea and dinner; read magazines; had a facial; saw what privileged people in third world countries do for leisure; and generally soaked up the "club culture". After three days, I was ready to climb the walls so I found a computer and logged onto world news.

My only intellectual stimulation was an invitation to speak at the Rotary Club in Karachi. I was to speak of my involvement in interfaith outreach in Canada. On the day of my talk, I donned my public speaker cap and checked my notes for signs of blasphemy. I had been warned not to venture into deep water. I think my family was concerned that I might say something controversial and spoil their social standing. *Me, controversial?*

I was thrilled to see that a Canadian Rotarian from Trenton was visiting and came to hear me speak. Just as well; I think he was the only one among 50 other men and two women in the audience who appreciated and understood what I said. He announced I was a great ambassador for Canada, a comment that jarred with my audience because it is difficult for them to accept that I can be a pluralist practising Muslim and a caring Canadian simultaneously.

My topic was about human rights, tolerance and the importance of interfaith outreach post-9/11, especially with Christians and Jews whom we consider to be from the same Abrahamic root and people of the book. The only other woman in the audience (one was my sister who was so stressed over my address that she didn't eat her lunch) wrote me a note saying that I am wrong: Islam is the only true Abrahamic faith and no one else will find salvation. This is the religious mood of majority of Pakistanis, irrespective of their social or economic status - dangerously exclusivist and holier-than-thou.

My touch on tolerance was shattered to the core as soon as I left the Rotary event. Newspaper headlines screamed the daylight shooting of Daniel Pearl, and a Shia doctor, head of the Kidney Center, father of two and twentieth in a line of innocent Shia doctors massacred since January 2002. It felt like a personal blow. But worse than the act itself was the feedback and justification. Most people told me I was over-reacting because I've become too Westernized. "Pakistanis could never do this - it's aliens," they said. "You don't know - Daniel Pearl was a spy." I felt sick and caustically congratulated them for having advanced from "Zionist or Indian conspiracies" to this "artificial intelligence" idea.

The other section of the community, the common man on the street, is totally confused about supporting the liberal view of the present government and being labelled "secular" (which is like abuse) or following the hate-spewing Mullah in the mosque. The masses have been brainwashed into justifying terrorism and blame everyone else for the problems facing Pakistan today. In an atmosphere rampant with stereotypes of "the West", America is the common enemy of both the elite and the masses.

However, their hypocrisy and double standards are soon revealed as they flaunt their Western ideals. On Valentine's Day, the city of Karachi floated red balloons and even the simple flower vendor at the street corner was caught up in the hype, stringing together garlands of hearts. Kids at school wore red and parents blamed it all on the West.

Similarly, when they eat at McDonald's and Kentucky Fried Chicken, they still gripe at the West but have no qualms about vacationing in Florida or lining up for days so their two-year-old children can get admission at The Karachi Grammar school, a Western symbol that raises status. It is also a status symbol to send kids to The American School or spend millions of rupees to educate them in America.

While I'm deeply troubled and saddened by the lack of personal accountability in Pakistan, I continue to love my country of birth (like a spoilt child) and will return whenever I can. I only criticize because I care.

THOUGHTS ON THE DESTRUCTION OF MY HOMELAND

When will it end...this massacre and carnage -
the blood, sweat and tears of our young and old?

When will we learn to live without fear...embedded
deep in our soul - with blood turned cold?

When will we stop destroying each other...
victims of the enemy who has become bold?

When will we say...peace in my land -
I want to go home?

THEIR JIHAD IS NOT MY JIHAD
July 2002

Since September 11, 2001, I've been invited to many churches, schools and community centers to speak about Islam to non-Muslims. People curiously ask if I'm trying to convert others or get converted myself! I tell them it's neither: What I do is essentially "damage control".

With time, I thought this fleeting interest in Islam and Muslims would fade, like a passing fad. Much to my surprise, it hasn't and today, one year down the road, I still find myself doing the rounds, teaching Islam 101!

One of the most satisfying aspects of these sessions is the Q & A's; this is when real issues surface and the spectre of an unknown fear is put to rest. I usually start off by telling my listeners that no question is too controversial and no issue too contentious for me. Questions have ranged from the sublime to the ridiculous: "How many wives does your husband have?" to "What is the history of the turban in Islam?"

However, there is one serious question that is posed every time, in various formats: "Is violence a part of your faith and does it say, somewhere in your scripture, that suicide is an honourable act to be rewarded by God? Is killing non-Muslims a form of *jihad*?"

It concerns me that while I spend valuable time and energy informing non-Muslims about the true interpretation of *jihad* (moral, intellectual and spiritual striving) and that violence and suicide are forbidden in Islam, there are many people in positions of authority within the Muslim world who simultaneously promote and condone violence. These are Islamists who believe their *jihad* is physical violence against civilians seen to be their enemy; to blow themselves up for political aims and to rid the earth of non-Muslims.

Obviously, their *jihad* and my *jihad* are not the same. I believe the *jihad* preached and practised by the Messenger of Islam Mohammad is not the one being propagated by people who support the path of violence against civilians, or who encourage the destruction of lives through suicide bombings.

Muslims unanimously hold there is no greater example of conduct for us than the Prophet Mohammad. For the first twelve years of his mission, he actively pursued a policy of non-violence and arbitration. For the following ten years he participated in war only when he had to, but preferred mediation and non-violent confrontations. As well, during time of war, the Prophet imposed severe restrictions on his generals and armies about not harming civilians, the environment, places of worship, women or children. Adhering to the teachings of the Prophet, his family and followers also persevered in the tradition of non-violent peace keeping.

Hence, I tell my audience, throughout hundreds of years of the spread of Islam, there is no recorded history of suicide being used as a weapon. There are heart-rending traditions of sacrifice and valour as Muslims faced far graver threats and challenges than they are up against today, but history records no exemplary acts of suicidal destruction. This is a relatively new phenomenon, not necessarily specific to the Islamic world. Japanese Kamikaze pilots; "suicidal" military exploits of the defenders of the Alamo and Tamil Tigers are other examples. The rise of suicide bombing amongst Muslims is unsettling because many Muslim clerics and scholars, well versed in the Qur'an, remain ominously silent when it comes to condemning suicide bombers and acts of terrorism against civilians.

Suicide bombings challenge two fundamental principles of Islamic ethics: the prohibitions against suicide and the deliberate killing of non-combatants. The Qur'an states clearly that killing one person is like killing all of humanity and taking your own life is a sin.

Today, the Muslim world stays dangerously silent and from the same pulpits where hate is spewed comes the potent sanction of murderous missions. Young, impressionable Muslims, frustrated by their cause, are led to believe that suicide missions will take them straight to paradise. Some of these misguided youths are promised virgins in paradise as their reward. Keeping in mind these decrees are normally given by males, I call such promises wishful thinking!

While there is no doubt in my mind about the legitimacy of the Palestinian cause and the ongoing destruction of its people's lives and lands, there is still no parallel or justification for suicide bombings. Some argue that it is acceptable through the clause of reciprocity. But this thinking abrogates the moral and ethical teachings of Islam, which does not allow a people to stoop to the level of their enemies, but insists that Muslims must behave according to the tenets of their own faith, which gives clear and lucid guidelines.

Martyrdom is the will of God, not humans. It doesn't provide religious or political clout - in fact, it reduces the power of any just cause. Justice or "*adl*" is a key concept in the Qur'an. Justice is described as the avoidance of excess. There should be neither too much nor too little; hence, the use of scales as the emblems of justice. Lest anyone try to do too much or too little, the Qur'an points out that no human being can carry another's burden or attain anything without striving for it.

The dilemma faced by the Muslim world today is echoed in another valid query. Where do we draw our strength of conviction and who empowers us to speak out against extremist voices from the pulpit? My audience is usually amazed when I inform them that Islam gives each one of us the freedom to logically research and interpret the Qur'an with reason and intellect. This understanding has recently brought the voices of many Muslim modernists to the forefront, rallying the message, "Forward with the Qur'an" and insisting on the importance of independent thought, both at the collective level (in the form of "*Ijma*") and at the individual level (called "*ijtehad*"), as a means of freeing Muslim thought from the dead weight of outmoded traditionalism.

I add my voice to theirs, as we unflinchingly condemn those cults that practise and promote their own form of Islam and *jihad* rooted in ignorance, rituals and dogma.

If I, as a Muslim woman, could ever be empowered to pass a *fatwa* (religious decree), I would declare these cults outside the fold of Islam.

Somebody should.

ROLE OF MEDIA IN ESTABLISHING PEACE IN SOCIETY
November 2002

Peace is a natural and inherent need of human beings which prospers when there is harmony among friends, neighbours and strangers. Harmony is achieved through tolerance, communication and discourse and most of all, by upholding truth and justice.

A simple perspective is that peace is the absence of conflict. The UNESCO constitution makes note that since wars begin in the minds of men, it is in the minds of men that the defence of peace must be constructed.

Media fuels the upholding or wrecking of this peace.

Media thrives on conflict. If media was as concerned about peace as we are, there would be cameras all around to record the dialogues of peace that are going on across North America by people and organizations that are trying to build bridges of understanding and tolerance.

It is a sad fact that the media would be more interested in reporting on a war rally than a peace forum.

There is far more coverage of conflicts than there is of peace. There is a reason for that: media is not a natural phenomenon. Newspapers, news and opinions don't occur naturally; they are made as a result of human will, history, social circumstances, institutions and the conventions of one's profession.

Media is our biggest challenge in this century. It represents one of the most powerful institutions in a democratic society. Media plays a powerful and potent role in shaping attitudes and perceptions, in dictating ideas and moulding policy. Gerald Levin, The CEO of Time-Warner says, "It's up to media to lead society and humanity in the pursuit of justice, equality and progress."

You may well ask how.

I believe the answer is simple. Democracy depends on a free press. We need unbiased information to live our lives in peace and media is a key provider of information, so it is critical that this coverage, whether print or electronic, be fair and balanced. Western media can do amazing things. It has the political liberty to present all sorts of notions, to provide eccentric, aberrant and sometimes incorrect views. There is frequently little accountability and much leverage.

Take the story of the Washington sniper who brutally and knowingly killed eight innocent people. Yet the media didn't call him a terrorist. Which is the way it should have been reported.

Media doesn't use the same tolerance and understanding when it comes to the Muslim community. In his insightful expose of how Western media deals with Islamic issues, Professor Edward Said, author of *Covering Islam*, explains that the media consists largely of profit-seeking corporations and therefore, quite understandably, has an interest in promoting some images over others.

Closer to home, Haroon Siddiqui of The Toronto Star wrote in a column that writers and editors are being dictated by media owners. He says there is huge gap between media and consumers that needs to be tightened. The role of media in peacemaking, or rather the lack of it, has never been more apparent than after September 11, 2001. U.S. media blew September 11 events out of proportion and sensationalized the negative aspects of this event.

Even on our side of the border, I had many calls post-September 11 from journalists, TV stations and radio hosts, looking for sensational stories, for drama about anger and revenge, about violence and discrimination. They were disappointed with me because I always reminded them that September 11, despite its tragic impact, was certainly *not* the most tragic event in the history of the world. Thousands of innocent civilians are dying needlessly every day in other parts of the world and receive little or no recognition by media.

Secondly, I pointed out, there were many peace-making and bridge-building stories that have never been told.

But the media was looking for sensation - because news that is sensational, that shocks, is in the end, news that sells the publication.

As a result, many peace-making events all over the world were sidelined. For example, nowhere in mainstream media did we read that in Europe, soon after September 11, 2001, there was a peace gathering of many multi-faith spiritual leaders from around the world who prayed for universal peace.

As the first anniversary of September 11 rolled around, North American media was once again in the business of sensationalizing the event. I say North America media with intention, because the same is not true across the Atlantic. I've traveled across the Atlantic a few times since September 11, 2001 and news changes faster than aircrafts change time zones. News in Europe is more balanced and definitely less abrasive than in North America. In countries outside North America, the September 11 anniversary was used to commemorate Afghan victims, Iraqi children of war, African casualties of Aids and thousands of other innocent deaths. This was not the case here at home. While on the one hand we say violence begets violence, media makes no effort to downplay their role in perpetuating violence.

One of most potent weapons used by media is the war of words. Violent and confrontational terminology is key propaganda. A sad example of media's role in creating havoc is the disgusting remark made by American Baptist pastor Reverend Jerry Falwell during an interview conducted by CBS's *60 Minutes* on October 6, 2002. Falwell told reporter Bob Simon that he believed the Muslim who commits acts of violence in *jihad* does so with the approval of Mohammad. "I think Mohammad was a terrorist," Falwell said. "He - I read enough of the history of his life written by both Muslims and - and - non-Muslims, that he was a - a violent man, a man of war."

The remark itself was rude and repulsive enough to have been ignored, but media picked it up and it was on the newswire within hours. Adding insult to injury, *60 Minutes* decided to air the issue on the weekend, making a sensitive Muslim community even more defensive.

Thanks to Western media's irresponsible use of jingo-ism instead of journalism, Muslims today have been made synonymous with terrorism, fundamentalism and militancy, whereas the same epithets do not apply to those rogue states and people who have been actually engaged in the killing of civilians far longer than terrorism became a buzz word in media.

Obviously, peace falls off the table when one community is targeted by media. In an article titled *Hidden Meanings in Western Media's Language of Discourse*, Zafar Bangash, director of Crescent International, gives a pertinent example of the Afghan mujahideen. Bangash says that when the Afghans were battling the Soviets, the Western press referred to them as "freedom fighters". Once the Soviet army was banished, the Afghans became guerrillas. Now they are rebels and outlaws.

Kashmiri freedom fighters are called militants or separatists even though their state is recognized by the UN as disputed territory. How can a people who are not part of a country be called separatists while they struggle to secure their rights?

There are numerous other examples of media's role in creating conflict rather than perpetuating peace. I don't wish to focus only on the negative, so in all fairness, I think I should give you a recent example of a piece of media coverage that does promote peace.

In The Toronto Star recently, there was beautiful story about a Hindu in India, who owns a mosque and hires a Muslim Imam to perform prayers. The story talks about living in harmony and understanding. Now here is a story that promotes peace-making efforts and it does have an impact because I had a call from two journalists today, asking if I would comment on the story.

I consider myself to be very tolerant and since I work in media, I do have an understanding of how things work. However, my patience also wears thin when media knowingly and consistently puts a barricade in the peace process by promoting images and stories that are biased, ignorant and one-sided.

Since society depends on media, change will only come when truth and justice become the landmarks of a great media. We need this in Canada, where peace-making has been a long standing tradition.

JIHAD IN THE NEWSROOM
May 2003

In the post-9/11 America, Muslim-bashing has become the national pastime - which is fine to some extent if the Americans would only get their terminology correct. Although almost anyone who could correctly pronounce "al-Qaeda" became an authority overnight on Islam and Muslims, the self-declared experts and the media couldn't get most of the jargon right.

For example:

- In the U.S. news, Muslims were called *Islamics* or *Mohammedans*. Even a seasoned journalist like Walter Cronkite referred to us as *Muslimites*.
- One reporter got so confused between *hijab* (which is a head covering) and *jihad* (a struggle) that she reported a Muslim woman wearing a *jihad*!
- In Canada, when the media bash Muslims, at least they get their wording correct. September 11, with all its bleakness, has certainly put Islam on the map and I must say Canadian media has moved ahead with integrity and honesty. Not 100 percent accuracy, but in all fairness, Islam is confusing for many Muslims as well.

I'm not just criticizing the media, but actually indulging in some constructive analysis to give examples and make some recommendations. I feel qualified to do this because I am in the unique position of being a Muslim journalist who is also a woman and who works on both sides of the fence.

I gained valuable experience and objective insight by default. Thirteen years ago, when I came to Canada, I didn't intend to become a writer of stories about Islam and Muslims. Unfortunately, at that time there was very little coverage of Islam. When there was any, it was largely distorted. I found the majority of images that the public saw were those reflecting oil or turmoil. The terminology associated with Muslims was inflammatory and seditious. Hence, the stories that surfaced were stereotypical and superficial.

A case in point: when the media reported on the Muslim festival of Eid - which is the largest celebration of Muslims the world over - the images were always of men in a mosque with their heads down and butts in the air. I mean no disrespect to the fact that the men were praying, but what about the women, the children, the henna and clothes, the diversity and the colour that are all part of the wonderful time of Eid?

As a result of the Canadian media's half-hearted attempts to cover Islamic events, a balanced Muslim diversity or a strong Muslim identity never emerged. It is sad, considering Islam is a cultural heritage that spans over 1,400 years.

As a Muslim activist and feminist, I was especially appalled at the negative portrayal of Muslim women in media. I kept examining the women who were portrayed in the stories; they are not part of the mainstream Muslim world that I know of.

When Islamic conferences or meetings were covered, only the men were interviewed. Now, this may have been a problem with the Muslim community or a cultural issue, but the media wasn't doing much to change the status quo. So I took to heart what Nihad Awad of the Council on American/Islamic Relations says: *"Before we criticize, we must educate."*

In 1999, I put together a resource kit for media called Muslim Women and Media which listed professional Muslim women as contacts. This kit reflected results of a poll and quoted Muslim women, especially young Canadian Muslim women, saying they would like to be asked to comment upon mainstream issues like the environment, elections and education.

I tried to empower media to reflect Muslims in the mainstream, not just in ethnic or religious stories. There is a fine line between culture and faith. Every story that has a Muslim in it is not always an ethnic or faith-related story.

Recently, The Toronto Star carried a special section on cottage country. My cottage story would have been part of that, except that my editor cut it. The editor said my story lacked magical, mystical, ethnic content. I tried. Truly, I incorporated everything from my nose ring to henna, but for Pete's sake, how ethnic can a true blooded Canadian cottage story be? The whole point of my story was that South Asians are not cottage people!

Through this exercise of trying to separate myth and reality, culture and faith, I learned that it is imperative to create awareness, both in the newsroom as well as within the community. This is what I believe I do best.

Why is awareness needed in the newsroom? Because that is where the story begins, where the decisions are made. If there is no diversity in the newsroom, then the result is sloppy and half-hearted. For example, when the female genital mutilation story broke (which is clearly not part of the faith, but a cultural practice), I called to ask The Globe and Mail if there was diversity training within newsrooms to handle a sensitive issue. The response was that there is no need for diversity training.

The fact is the media is no longer dealing with Islam *and* the West - it's Islam and Muslims *in* the West. Recent statistics show that Eastern religions and especially Islam are the fastest growing faiths in Canada. The number of Muslims has doubled in past 10 years, so it is obviously a demographic necessity and practicality to know more about a people that are an integral part of the community.

Canada's House of Commons' standing committee on foreign affairs launched a study on *Canada's Relations with the Countries of the Muslim World*. The study says that fundamental to enhancing those relations is improving our collective understanding of Islam and its peoples. An important step forward is to see the Muslim world's remarkable but often overlooked diversity and history.

In the past, media had an excuse because when they needed to find a person in the Muslim community to comment on a current issue, there were only a handful of people on their roster. It was always the same Imam of the same mosque commenting on women's rights or the lack thereof. I think the media lapped it up because it made for sensational if inaccurate stories. But today, with over 600,000 Muslims living across Canada (more than 400,000 of them reside in Ontario) from over 60 countries around the world, the expectation is that media would be able to get sound bites for almost any topic from a very diverse group, something that would be reflective of the real world of Islam.

The challenge for reporters is the Muslim community's fear of media, a mistrust that is rightly earned. Being chewed up and spit out by Ontario current affairs television show host Michael Coren can create long-term ego damage. I've been there so I know it's not easy to open up to a reporter who may be uniformed or poorly prepared for the interview.

Understanding the level of mistrust, in 2000, I created a guide for the Canadian Muslim community on how to be proactive with media at various levels.

It is interesting that other minority communities have also faced similar issues. In 2001, I worked as a consultant with the Periodical Writers Association of Canada (PWAC) and organized four workshops across Canada, which discussed racial barriers for minority writers. The resulting report for PWAC, entitled "Challenging Racial Barriers in Journalism", cites examples from the aboriginal and black communities illustrating how they have encountered barriers with media.

One recommendation made by the journalists at these PWAC workshops was for media and the offended community to interact more. I've tried to facilitate such meetings, but I must admit that sometimes they backfire and become media bashing sessions, which do not help the cause. Fortunately, there have been positive developments: CTV has created a diversity round table and The Toronto Star has established a diversity section and editor.

There is no doubt the Muslim community needs to be more accessible and available. Let's look at some of the hottest stories dealing with Muslims and how they were reported. Before the American war on Iraq, there was 9/11. What a mess the media made of that. In the mad scramble to feed the public's need for information, it appeared the media interviewed anyone who knew where Afghanistan was on the map. Very few of the so-called experts on Islam had read the history and politics of the region, or knew much about the faith. Afghan women, who were front and centre in the war, were usually overlooked by reporters. Most journalists missed the true essence of the bravery, heroism and strength of these women.

What the mainstream media needs to do is check accuracy, do their homework and become more balanced. It's alright to criticize Muslims when they are involved in political acts of sabotage, but at the same time, it is imperative to give the cause and effect. A story with no history or background remains superficial and unfair to the community.

The New York Times and The Washington Post have recently shown examples of balanced editorials where both Muslims and non-Muslims are discussing the state of the Muslim world without calling names. It is refreshing and allows Muslims to acknowledge the villains in their midst, without becoming defensive.

It is important, therefore, to build bridges and partnerships and to invite communication and dialogue *before* an event occurs that requires input from diverse communities. The media needs to understand that faith and culture are two separate issues. Muslims, like every other group of people, are multilayered. They are involved in every aspect of community life. There are grey areas. Not all stories dealing with Muslims are faith-related.

ARE OUR CIVIL LIBERTIES AT STAKE?
November 2003

Rights and liberties are issues close to Muslims' hearts and minds. Muslims today find themselves caught between a rock and a hard place: the rock being an ideology gone mad – the likes of Osama bin Laden and his mentors; the hard place being the powers that support puppet regimes. Moderate Muslims like me who want to differentiate our faith from extremist Muslims' twisted ideologies are facing increasing resistance. Sadly, it is in the interest of imperialistic powers to keep the general population of the world confused so the average public views Muslims as terrorists.

Here is an anecdote: In New York's Central Park, a dog was attacking a small boy. A young man passing by rescued the boy. A New York Times reporter who was nearby saw the incident and was impressed. He approached the rescuer and said the headline next day would read, "Courageous New Yorker risks life to save child". The man said he was not from New York. The reporter said, "No problem, the headline will read: Valiant American makes daring move to save child". The man said he's not American but a visitor from Pakistan. The headlines in The New York Times the next day read: "Pakistani terrorist attacks dog - al-Qaeda links being investigated".

When I first heard this, it was as a joke. Alas, it's no longer funny, as this perception has become reality. The consensus is: if it looks like a duck, walks like a duck, talks like a duck - it must be Muslim!

An excessive, overzealous security agenda since September 11 has made Muslims feel anxiety, fear, alienation, betrayal and disillusionment. In the hours after the events of 9/11, scattered hate and racist attitudes were directed at Muslim Canadians on the streets of our cities, in schoolyards and workplaces, from strangers and from vandals who attacked places of worship. Ironically, racism combined with total ignorance rose to the surface, which led to hoodlums burning a Hindu temple and an attack on a Sikh man in Canada.

Next came mass detentions of Arabs and Muslims - dozens here in Canada, thousands south of the border, incarcerated under a cloak of secrecy. Secret detentions, secret hearings, secret evidence, secret names, secret numbers of those arrested.

Canada's Bill C-36 followed and quickly became law, allowing, among other things, preventative detentions and forced testimony - abominations in a free society. While some argued, rightly, that the Anti-terrorism Act did not single out Arabs and Muslims and is directed at all Canadians, we Arabs and Muslims nevertheless felt the act targeted a specific community. We were not wrong.

Civil liberties and human rights are the bricks that build a society. Once we allow them to start crumbling and decaying, the damage never stops.

The Jewish community is not new to persecution and hate crimes and it was during tough times like the ones I've mentioned that our friends in faith stretched out a hand of support and assisted Canadian Muslims in dealing with hate crimes. I worked with B'nai Brith to counter some of the issues with which we were dealing.

In the months following 9/11, there were reported abuses by law enforcement, and Canadian Security Intelligence Service in particular, which seemed to cast too wide a net. While on this terrorist fishing expedition, CSIS conducted intrusive interrogations of innocent people and, most damaging, pressured ordinary Arab Canadians to act as spies and inform on their friends and colleagues.

Media did not help. Unqualified "experts" on Islam and Muslims gave ignorant and uninformed opinions as they tried to paint all Muslims with the terrorist brush. The stereotypes and racist overtones put forward by some in the mainstream media confirmed the permissibility of singling out Arabs and Muslims for suspicious treatment. The message was: they are guilty by association; suspect by nature of their ethnicity and religion; therefore, an acceptable object of hate.

There were heartrending incidents, like a Muslim boy in Western Ontario who was hung by his non-Muslim friends. Police cars circled certain Ontario mosques at all hours of the day and Muslim women in *hijab* were abused verbally and physically.

This is all in the past, but I believe the situation today is worse. The Toronto Police Department records a 66 percent increase in hate crimes. We are currently seeing our civil rights being trampled. Following September 11, 2001, the Government of Canada approved sweeping new powers for the Royal Canadian Mounted Police, allowing officers to search homes without warrants, and gain access to a wider range of personal information. The Immigration and Refugee Law was also given the provision that allowed them to detain people based on reasonable suspicion.

As a result of this unleashed power, 24 Pakistani students were arrested for the crime of misrepresenting themselves to Immigration and detained for being enrolled as students at the Ottawa Business College, which turned out to be a scam. If being an illegal immigrant is a crime, then hundreds more in Canada should be rounded up and hounded like these young Pakistanis, who were first held in a maximum security facility where they were physically and psychologically abused by other inmates and later removed to solitary confinement.

The RCMP claimed they removed five truckloads of material from these destitute students. The material turned out to be 35 mattresses, hardly evidence leading to terrorists or weapons of mass destruction.

Some tactics now in practice are violations of the Charter of Rights: individuals are told there are a number of unanswered questions concerning them and that they "ought to come in" but that RCMP officers won't speak to them if they bring their own lawyers. The effect on our community is palpable. Even people like me, who have been eternal optimists, feel the cold creeping in.

Recently, a Canadian television studio called to invite me on a panel discussion regarding the aftermath of September 11. The journalist wanted to discuss my position regarding the rights and freedoms of Muslims in Canada. I made my stance very clear. He said, "But if September 11 had taken place in your country, Pakistan, they would have massacred the criminals." I told him the reason many of us came to Canada is for freedom and democracy, which we don't find in many parts of the third world.

If we are denied those basic human rights as Canadian citizens, and if Canada can't protect us, then what is the point in living here as loyal Canadians? Like our Japanese-Canadian counterparts during World War II, we, too, have become victims of psychological internment.

I am troubled that these days, anyone with a Muslim name or a beard and brown skin is questioned at border crossings, airports and even in their own neighbourhoods. After the 1995 Oklahoma bombing, were people ever stopped at an airport because their name was Timothy?

I have two sons, aged 18 and 20. They grew up here and are as Canadian as the goose or moose. They are unaware of the politics of power and are innocent bystanders. However, my husband and I have stopped them from traveling to the U.S. for the time being, until things blow over.

A member of parliament visiting from the United Kingdom remarked that he noted no mention of the civil rights issues regarding the 24 Pakistanis in any of the major newspapers. It is a shame for sure.

LOYALTY TOWARDS OUR ADOPTED LAND
December 2003

Abdulrahman Khadr's picture on the front page of The Toronto Star touches my heart. Bright-eyed, clean cut and 20, the same age as my older son, he looks like an average Canadian youth. But something seems to be amiss.

While my two boys learned to load the dishwasher, Khadr learned to load an assault rifle. While, much to my annoyance, my boys played violent video games, Khadr was actually living among people who practise violence against women and minorities. When I proudly took my kids on their first trip to Disneyland, Khadr was proudly sent to a training camp in Afghanistan. When my boys went to Sunday school in Brampton to learn their Islam, Khadr was being taught in a land far away.

There's something terribly wrong with this picture, and I'm trying to make sense of it.

My concern as a Muslim mother is that Khadr seems to take all this in stride. He says that he and an older brother took training because it was "a normal thing that everybody does in Afghanistan". That may be so. But is it normal for Canadian Muslims to send their kids to learn violence and destruction in a camp thousands of miles away?

When my children came as young kids to Canada, their father and I taught them about loyalty to their adopted land and respect for the Canadian Charter of Rights and Freedom, which is not at odds with our Muslim values. We also made it a point to take them back regularly to Pakistan, our country of origin, so that they would know their roots and become culturally aware.

At one point, my younger son, at age 18, wanted to join the Canadian armed forces. I asked him, "If Canada were by chance to go to war against the land of your parents' birth, where would your loyalties lie?" Without the flicker of an eyelash, he said, "Canada, of course." I didn't reprimand him because he "stands on guard" for Canada.

Much of the onus and responsibility about what happens with our children's future lies with the parents. In a country like Canada, there are ample opportunities to help those in distress and those living in war-torn countries through valid means. Doctors Without Borders is a perfect example. I feel sorry for Muslim youth like Khadr, who haven't been taught that Islam means peace and submission to the will of God - not submission to the call for violence being spouted by some malicious Mullahs.

If parents are naïve and don't watch what their children are absorbing, then unfortunately, we will have produced many Khadrs in our society.

It's easy to become prey to the emotional call for a physical *jihad* as many Muslim youth, born and bred in England, have done in the recent past. They were sucked into the vortex of an ideology gone mad and never told that the larger *jihad* is that of tolerance and understanding. I often wonder about those who entice youth to commit suicide bombing. We don't see any of those who preach suicide bombing throwing themselves in front of a bus.

Khadr's case is a huge wake up call for all Canadian Muslims. This could happen to our kids. But we hope it won't because we are vigilant about what they learn, about teaching them inherent Muslim values and applying them in the Canadian context.

As the web of hatred increases from East to West and people find trouble with religion, we try to build bridges and steer our family away from the ritual to the spiritual, finding truth not only in the Qur'an but in messages of peace and justice emanating from all faiths.

Hate and racism are taught at home and children take example from their parents. From the fall of the Buddha statues in Afghanistan to the burning of libraries in Iraq, we as a family have lobbied against injustice and shared our joys and sorrows with our friends of all faiths. We enjoy a *langar* (meal) in a Sikh Gurdwara on Dixie Road in Mississauga, Ontario as much as we appreciate answering tough questions about Islam in Canadian churches or synagogues.

I wonder if those who have enormous resentment in their hearts ever had the pleasure of driving along the "spiritual strip" on Bayview Avenue in Toronto where a Chinese temple, Christian churches, a Zoroastrian temple, a mosque and a synagogue stand side by side. If they did, they would be awed by the beauty and tolerance that lies at the heart of Canada.

REALITY CHECK ON SECURITY CHECKS
February 2004

I went for my flu shot this morning, registered at the reception desk and sat to wait my turn. About five minutes later I noticed that four people (all white) who had come after me got called in while I still waited. "Aha," I thought, "there's racial profiling going on here."

My conclusion had much to do with my reading the newspaper, which abounds with material on this hot topic. However, I decided to stay cool and after the fourth person went ahead of me, I asked the receptionist what the matter was. She was mortified to discover that she had missed my name on the list and apologized so profusely that I felt embarrassed.

The incident made me realize that it's easy to make an issue about racial profiling. In this case, it was simple human error. Racial profiling, racism and discrimination are real concerns but they are sometimes fuelled by our own perceptions.

Some form of racial profiling exists in every part of the world - I've lived in the Arab world long enough to know that priorities there are Whites, Arabs and Asians in terms of jobs, visas and attitude. Some Middle Eastern countries are paranoid about security and use very elementary methods of implementing them. But many of us accept these restrictions because we *expect* them.

Rohinton Mistry, a respected Canadian writer, cancelled his trip to the U.S. because he felt American security inspections were degrading. The Indian-born Canadian, who is not Muslim, claimed he endured "unbearable humiliation" due to racial profiling. Mistry remarked, "The way you look, where you were born....will determine how you will be treated at certain airports."

Yes, he is absolutely right, but those "certain airports" are not only in the U.S.

I'll never forget my last visit to Saudi Arabia. They treat you like dirt if you're Asian. I remember standing in a long line with two kids, hungry and tired while the customs officer sipped tea and chatted with his friends, calling out those passengers who had British or American passports. When we finally made it to the front of the line, he left our passports on the counter and went away for a break without so much as an explanation. Our luggage was searched and the cover torn off a book because it had the photo of a woman. The attitude was so harsh that as a Muslim, I vowed that the only reason I would ever go there again would be to visit the holy shrines.

On my return from Pakistan recently, I had an unnerving experience at Karachi airport. My luggage was searched by two men, put through an x-ray machine and machine bound by a metal strip. Then I went through a strict immigration check where I was photographed. Two steps later, I was stopped by an obnoxious and arrogant Federal Investigation Agency agent who rudely questioned my status as a woman traveling alone. He wanted to confiscate my Canadian passport till I told him whether I had a husband or father in Canada. When I protested loudly that it was none of his business, I nearly got arrested. Being surrounded by a dozen gun-toting, rough-looking army guys is no joke! I was shaken to the core.

Just before boarding the plane, we went through security again and this time, a woman felt me all over as part of the body search! I couldn't yell racism because these were my own people. I justified this horrific experience by saying they were doing their job of handling security the only way they knew how.

I returned to Toronto via London where there was intense screening and long lines, shoes on one side and passengers on the other, while the customs officers searched all hand luggage. I went through all sorts of machines along with other passengers. The British are not rude, but quite brusque. No one complained.

People are complaining that U.S. security is stringent. However, it wasn't too long ago that there was an invasion of security in America, where thousands of civilians were brutally killed in a non-combative attack. The terrorists were from different parts of the world.

A few months later a shoe bomber nearly blew up a plane. Why is it so difficult for the average traveler to accept that the Americans have a right to tighten their security and obviously target those of ethnic origin who come from countries that the terrorists boasted to be from?

In the past year, I've made numerous trips to the U.S. and have never been mistreated at a US airport. I've been delayed and searched, but not singled out despite my ethnic appearance, nose ring and birthplace on the passport. Recently, my husband and I were in Denver, Colorado, which has a huge airport. Prior to our departing flight, everyone had to go through intense security. It took 45 minutes and was extremely well organized. Security personnel were polite and well informed; they told everyone what was happening at every step and said please and thanks. If they had to search your person, they actually made a statement before touching you.

There was only one seat on the flight back to Toronto so my husband had to stay back and for a moment I was worried. He sports a beard, looks like he is from the Middle East and was born in Pakistan so he has "the profile". Sohail told me he couldn't have been treated better. Not only did airport personnel work at getting him on another flight to Toronto right away, they apologized profusely for something that wasn't their fault. He had to come via Chicago, another huge airport where security is very rigid. However, Sohail went through the process with many others and he argues that he was the one whom most security personnel apologized to. Likely, the polite treatment was because Sohail refrained from letting off his frustration in being delayed onto the security personnel, recognizing they were doing the best they could.

There are exceptions to the rule, of course. Even in normal times, there are bigots and people with a personal axe to grind. Racism and discrimination do exist. These, however, are not normal times for the U.S. While clarifying that I have no love lost for President George W. Bush or American foreign policies, I believe the U.S. has reason to be cautious. At security checks, if one observes carefully, without a chip on the shoulder, then it becomes apparent that black, brown and white people are randomly stopped and searched. If those of Middle Eastern descent are searched more than others, then maybe the U.S. has good reason to do so. If the angst against airport security checks in America is so great, we can either get used to it or stop going there.

A CALL TO ARMS FOR MODERATE MUSLIMS
April 2004

The recent raids in Britain that resulted in the arrests of nine men of Pakistani heritage and the subsequent raid at the home of a Canadian in Ottawa are cause for grave concern. Concern, not just about the credibility of the Royal Canadian Mounted Police, (after their bungling over the arrest of 19 Pakistani students where no terrorism charges were proven), but concern about the future of Muslims in Canada.

As a Muslim Canadian, my work within and outside my community has suddenly become an enormous challenge.

The other day, I was invited to address a church group in Etobicoke, Ontario as part of my interfaith outreach. The topic, naturally, was Islam. The audience was familiar with the basics of Islam. They were more interested in knowing how I, as a Canadian Muslim, experience religion in my life and how Islam relates to other faiths.

I spoke about the Islam that I love and respect, the Islam that I learned and practised in Pakistan and now in Canada; the Islam of the Qur'an and Prophet Muhammad that instilled respect for all humanity; that is a moral and ethical code and, above all, values justice. I also talked about my children who are caring, believing Canadian Muslims.

Afterward, people asked me about diversity within Islam. I said there are various paths that lead to God - the same God of the Jews and Christians whom we call Allah.

One person asked me how difficult it is to practice Islam in Canada. I told her that as a Muslim woman I can practice my faith more easily in Canada than I can in many Muslim countries where extremism and a warped ideology have taken over the norms of respect and tolerance. I pointed out that I'm a Sunni married to a Shia and noted that my kids are fondly called "Sushis."

At the end of my presentation, a perturbed looking woman, a teacher, asked to speak to me privately. She explained that she has many Muslim students so she decided to learn about Islam by attending classes at a Toronto mosque.

"Everything they told me at the mosque is at odds with what you are saying here today...you talk about similarities between Muslims and "people of the book"; they said there is no point of reference for Muslims and non-Muslims. When I asked about the different sects - because my students are from diverse denominations - they said that Shias, Ismailis and Ahmedis are not Muslims. You talk about finding liberation and freedom as a woman within Islam, but at the mosque the women weren't even allowed to speak."

"You've blown my mind. Why isn't a narrative like yours being heard all over Canada?"

I replied that my views are those of the silent majority who unfortunately are just that - silent. But after the spiralling events of Madrid, Britain and now Ottawa, we can no longer remain silent.

So, my concerns and my questions to the Canadian Muslim community are: Why is the narrative of extremism taking precedent over voices of sanity and sense? How is the culture of extremism being kept alive in Canada. What are we going to do about it?

Never in the history of the world as I know it has there been such extensive dissection, dialogue and discussion about a faith as there has been about Islam, post-September 11, 2001.

Muslims have been stripped naked by the likes of Christian fundamentalists Jerry Falwell and Pat Robertson and political interviewer Oriana Fallaci. Even some local Muslims made a name for themselves by pointing out the trouble with Islam.

In this atmosphere rampant with distrust and fear, people became confused. As a Muslim involved in doing damage control, it was time to go back to the books and read, which is the first message of the Qur'an.

In the immediate aftermath of 9/11, many Muslim scholars and intellectuals spoke out. We were exposed to books and writings by leading-edge thinkers such as Khaled Abou el Fadl, Dr. Abdul Aziz Sachedina and Canadian professor Amir Hussain. More importantly for me, women's voices were being heard, such as Amina Wadud.

It was prime time for interfaith outreach and the United Church of Canada took the lead in Muslim-Christian solidarity by working on a document called *That We May Know Each Other*. We started to build bridges of understanding and fellow Canadians realized that it's not about Islam and the West but Muslims *in* the West. These Muslims are under massive pressure since 9/11 and have faced a severe backlash.

But other communities have reached out and vice-versa. Recently, when the Jewish community was victimized by hate-fuelled vandalism,

Muslims stood by them and supported them in their cause. There was hope on the horizon.

That hope is dashed every time a Muslim is allowed to indulge in hate propaganda and polemics. There is a problem when my university-going son asks why Muslim student associations spout venom against non-Muslims. There is cause for concern when anti-American rhetoric becomes the flavour of the month and justifies a different kind of polemic.

All this has to stop. But how?

The Muslim Council of Britain has taken the unprecedented step of writing to every British mosque, urging people to help in the fight against terror. A Rand report published recently says that Americans must give precedent to progressive and moderate Muslim voices.

In Canada we have to do the same. But this effort must come from both sides. Officials dealing with terrorism have to ensure they have evidence and that due judicial processes are followed. They have to build alliances with Muslims and create credibility.

At the same time, it is imperative for Muslims to speak out against human rights violations and take urgent action to see that terrorism, extremism and anti-Western propaganda are eliminated.

In Canada, we must take back the mosques to ensure the voices of reasonable Muslim men and women are heard over the stringent calls for a physical *jihad*.

Our *jihad* is to ensure that Canada remains a safe and peaceful environment for Muslims and non-Muslims alike.

THREE WEDDINGS AND A FUNERAL
MAY 2004

At a Muslim wedding in Markham recently, about 350 guests faced an embarrassing situation. The self-proclaimed Imam (spiritual leader) who was invited by the hosts to say a few words got totally carried away and gave a long, offensive monologue. First, he publicly denounced non-Muslims for lacking family values; he asked the groom thrice if he wanted to escape from the wedding; furthermore he informed the bride that she does not have the right to step outside the house or give anything to her family without her husband's permission. He reinforced these "rules" by mentioning hellfire and brimstone. There was no talk of love, respect and consideration between the couple. The guests were stunned, the couple looked shocked and a few people stood up in protest but no one contradicted the speaker. Obviously, they had no idea what to do.

Upon inquiring how a balanced, educated family could allow someone to spew such vitriol, the hosts explained their agreement with the speaker had been for him to repeat the marriage sermon of Prophet Mohammad as done traditionally at Muslim weddings (which is short and simple, highlighting the sanctity and beauty of marriage). They had no clue that he would indulge in histrionics.

Muslim marriages do not necessitate a sermon to be recited as part of the religious ceremony. The requirement is for *aqd*, which is solemnization of the contract through offering and acceptance with full and free consent of the parties concerned, two witnesses and a gift from the groom to the bride. A respected community member may be invited to say a few words, which could range from relevant verses of the Qur'an to Sufi poetry by Rumi. A public celebration to bless the union is considered to be *Sunnah* (practice of the Prophet) and this celebration can be as festive as the family wishes it to be. Weddings are not meant to be dark and dreary as some dysfunctional Mullahs indicate, when they pose themselves as reformers, exhorting misogynist theories supported by useless traditions and ranting about "Western corruption", which is absolutely contrary to the faith.

It seems these people have taken it upon themselves to use occasions like weddings and funerals to endorse their personal views. Recently, at a funeral in Toronto, the Imam who was asked to pray for the soul of the departed blasted the Supreme Court of Canada for 30 minutes on the issue of same sex marriages! Wrong time, wrong place.

However, misuse of power by religious leaders is not unique to the Muslim community. In Santa Fe, New Mexico, a family has filed a lawsuit against their local Catholic church over a funeral mass in which the priest allegedly said their relative was a "lukewarm" Catholic and was going to hell. (The Toronto Star, July 18, 2003). Religious exploitation seems to have taken the world by storm.

At a second wedding in Toronto, the Imam lectured women about their marital duties, interpreted in the most conservative framework, with no mention that Prophet Mohammad's wife, Khadija, a successful businesswoman, had sent a proposal of marriage to him. He then informed the guests that they shouldn't befriend Jews and Christians and proceeded to point out the faults of the "infidels" until the young bride burst into tears and told him that most of her friends present at the event were Jews and Christians! So much for joy!

Our only hope as a thriving and contributing Canadian Muslim community lies in removing the power of those who distort the faith. Some young Muslims took the initiative of doing just that at a recent wedding. The bride and her brother organized the reception, informing the parents that their only contribution would be their credit card! There was no sermon. The occasion reflected the best of both Muslim and Western worlds. Point of note is the families of the bride and groom are quite traditional, so a simple religious ceremony had been performed earlier at a mosque with immediate family in attendance. Later, family and friends were invited to a mixed reception where *hijab* and henna mingled with halter dresses and high heels to the strains of traditional music. Friends and families blessed the couple in an atmosphere filled with joy - finally, a Muslim-Canadian wedding with some feeling.

WHAT LED TO THE LONDON BOMBINGS?
July 2005

The heart-rending loss of humanity in the wake of the London, England bombings is a tragedy that affects all of us, Muslim and non-Muslim alike.

The blasts didn't come as a total surprise because the writing was on the wall. Despite the cause and effect theory which has been propounded extensively by commentators, this is a home-grown problem and it can only be solved within the community that allowed it to grow. That community is not necessarily a religious community, but a multicultural community like ours here in Canada.

I say this with feeling because I am a Pakistani Muslim woman with two sons, the same age as the suicide bombers in London. The difference is that my sons are secular in their public life and soundly knowledgeable and religious in their private life. They have grown up in an environment of respect for interfaith and life. More importantly, they know how to balance both.

Early this year, my 20-year-old son, Saif, went to Birmingham, England to visit a friend he hadn't seen in a long time. When he returned he was quite perturbed. Upon probing, he confessed that he found his counterparts in England very disturbing in their religious ideology. Attending Friday prayer in a mosque, Saif was shocked by the fire and brimstone being spouted from the pulpit.

Later, he took a drive with his Muslim friend. They had a flat tire. My son noted they had just passed a gas station and suggested they take the car there to be fixed. To his surprise and dismay, the three British-Muslim boys with him said they would rather walk than take their business to a non-Muslim. They proceeded to try and indoctrinate my son about the ills of the West and how important it was not to integrate with locals. Saif was alarmed by the attitude of these young Muslims and found they were totally dishonest and disconnected with the reality of living in the West and with any values of assimilation.

I've seen this trend on my visits to Britain. There is a growing sense of frustration in the youth and it's dangerous. The London bombings are symbolic of this malaise.

Granted, there are many political, economic and social factors that come into play when we talk about terrorism today. These are not part of a hidden agenda any more. Anyone with half a brain is aware that the war in Iraq and the American foreign policy play strong roles in any reaction to the West. But it does not, and will never, justify death of innocents.

Can this happen in Canada? Maybe. Unless we wake up and smell the coffee. By "we", I don't mean only Muslims, although public opinion would like to make this exclusively an Islamic problem. When the bubble of complacency bursts, it affects all of us. Before we are left blaming each other, let's try and look at solutions.

I don't believe technical surveillance, airport checks, limiting immigration and picking up bearded Muslim men at random is the solution. Obviously, targeting one community is not the answer, either.

The solution lies with parents and guardians, peers and advisors, teachers and religious institutions. All of us need to be more vigilant about the kind of rhetoric being spouted, about the ideology of hate being exported into Canada, about Muslim youth becoming targets for al-Qaeda recruiters in places of education and worship. Most important perhaps, is teaching our youth to raise their voices in condemning all acts of violence and being aware about what is going on around them.

Last month, two of the largest centres of Islamic learning, Al Azhar in Egypt and Qum in Iran, issued a joint *fatwa*, stating that suicide bombing is a sin - an unacceptable act under any circumstance. In Amman, Jordan, more than 170 Muslim scholars, thinkers and historians who gathered for an international Islamic conference agreed to forbid labelling anyone with apostasy, condemning extremists who use hate ideology to fire up sentiments against others.

In response to those who want to know where moderate Muslims are hiding, let me inform them we are alive and well and working around the clock to undo the damage done by 30 years of indoctrination of an ideology of hate. Where and how this ideology was invited into the West is whole other story, but let it suffice to say that we work hard to get our voices heard. But like every other extremist movement, the loudest voices are those of the damned.

The bombing in London was close to home. My brother-in-law was on the train just before the one that was bombed. We were terrified till we knew he was safe. Similarly, hundreds of other relatives, friends and loved ones must also have worried themselves sick. In the wake of the attack, many families mourn their dead and so do we.

Our loss increases as we mourn not only the dead and wounded, we also mourn the living who have lost their souls. Before the soul of our faith, our youth, our loved ones, is sucked away by the devil in disguise, let us join hands for the greatest of all *jihads* - the struggle to respect the dignity of human life.

PART 2

GENDER JIHAD -
A STRUGGLE FOR WOMEN'S RIGHTS

"I shall not lose sight of the labour of any of you who labours in my way, be it man or woman; each of you is equal to the other"
The Qur'an

☙❧

THE SILENT REVOLUTION – WOMEN IN ISLAM
January 2002

The latest statistics on religion in Canada show that Eastern religions, Buddhism, Hinduism and Islam, are the fastest growing religions in Canada. The number of Muslims has doubled in the last decade.

Canada's House of Commons' standing committee on foreign affairs has launched a study on *Canada's Relations with the Countries of the Muslim World*. Fundamental to enhancing those relations is improving our collective understanding of Islam and its peoples.

Women represent more than 50 percent of that society, so their rights and privileges need to be addressed clearly and articulately.

Awareness of Muslim women's issues is clearly required. The question is, where will that awareness come from? You can't depend on the media to remove the negative stereotypical images of Muslim women or to learn about the real lives led by Muslim women worldwide. The images that you see in print or on CNN are not even remotely reflective of the lives of Muslim women in general. The media, unfortunately, has been responsible for presenting a garbled image of Muslim women, providing negative portrayals and sensationalist propaganda for the masses. Books like *Not Without my Daughter* or *Princess* don't portray the lives of the majority of Muslim women, but are based on limited personal experience.

There is enormous plurality in the Muslim world and major variations in the traditions of African, Arab, Asian or European Muslims. Muslims come from almost 60 countries of the world so they reflect a rich cultural mosaic. Like the differences in our language, food and clothing from one region to another, Muslim women are diverse. Stereotypical assumptions about us as women in black shrouds are as inaccurate as the assumption that all Canadian women are personified by the bikini-clad photos in The Toronto Sun newspaper.

Western press tends to view Muslim women by the way they dress more specifically than who they are as a people. Therefore, they have reduced the Muslim female identity to a piece of cloth - the veil. It is rare to have a conversation about Muslim women without using the four letter word, "veil."

Modern, successful Muslim women are routinely excluded from mainstream media. It's unfortunate the achievements of many Muslim women today are buried under an avalanche of misinformation by media that projects them as third class citizens or non-contributing members of society. The media can't seem to comprehend that a head covering doesn't make anyone brain-damaged and that the real issue is freedom of dress (especially in North America, where women can have the liberty to bare their chests, a head covering worn as a cultural or religious symbol certainly shouldn't bother them).

A majority of Muslim women who cover their heads do so by choice and we must respect that choice. Having said this, I should mention that a cult like the Taliban, which forced women to cower under black shrouds and beat them if their skin showed, are not part of the Islam we are talking about.

In many areas of the Middle East, the head scarf is a cultural symbol. My Arab Christian friend told me that in Palestine, Christian women cover their heads. So on my recent trip to Dubai in the Arabian Gulf, I was struck by the fact that the women are covered, confident, content and in some ways, more liberated on a spiritual and intellectual level than Western women. They do everything we do in North America and more. They work outside their homes; they are educators, politicians and leaders. They also sit in a tent by the beach in the evening and smoke flavoured hubbly-bubbly - something we can only dream of!

My experience in Dubai reiterated what I've always believed: that Muslim women are movers and shakers, as well as very actively engaged in the societies where they reside. For example, the majority of graduate-school students in Qatar are women. The Iranian parliament has more women members than the U.S. Senate. Currently, there is major discussion and debate taking place amongst the educated and professional women of Iran about their rights.

According to a book *Islam and Gender*, written by social anthropologist Ziba Mir-Hosseini, a paradox has occurred in Iran where women are questioning the clergy about their rights and are looking for ways to prove the general message of the Qur'an is one of egalitarianism.

Fatima Mernissi, a Moroccan sociologist, activist and author of many books regarding women in Islam, was born in 1940 in Egypt, the same time feminism emerged in her country. The two have continued to exist side by side. In the 1930's, Huda al Sharawi was a radical feminist, even by today's standards. But feminism, like all other movements in Islam, has its boundaries. Since Islam is a way of life, everything we do is ruled by parameters laid down for us in the Qur'an and the traditions of the Prophet. So if I were asked if my brand of feminism translates into bra-burning, then I would have to say, no.

Inspirational, ground-breaking Muslim women can be found closer to home. British author Virginia Woolf wrote, "*as a woman I have no country - as a woman my country is the whole world.*" This stands true of the Muslim women who left their homes in South Asia and the Middle East, and came as pioneers to Canada, a foreign and cold land, in the early 1900's. They came to support their families, many of them with no language abilities and some who had never seen snow. But they went far north and weathered more than the winter. When the men failed to build a mosque, it was a small group of women from these early settlers that petitioned for the first mosque to be created in Edmonton. They went door to door on Jasper Avenue, convincing people to join in their campaign and in 1938, the first mosque in Canada, the al Rashid mosque, was named.

Dr. Lila Fahlman founded the first registered national Muslim women's organization, the Canadian Council of Muslim Women, which has been instrumental in helping Muslim women assimilate into Canadian life.

Since September 11, Muslims and especially Muslim women have been under a microscope. Front and centre have been Afghan women. Western feminists want to liberate rural Afghan woman by removing the *burka* (the black, head-to-toe outer covering), which to the feminists has become a symbol of repression. However, the Western feminists are totally unaware that thousands of Afghan women were very modernized, liberal and educated at Kabul University, which was an educational icon, until the time that the Taliban ruled out education from people's lives and plunged them back into the dark ages. For rural Afghan women, the *burka* was never their major focus of concern. Their priorities are more basic, like food, clothing, housing and most significantly, living free from violence.

However, recent articles in the Western media suggest the *burka* is of utmost importance for Afghan women. The media was bewildered when all Afghan women didn't shed their *burkas* and run out on the streets bareheaded, when the Taliban were defeated. Ironically, when asked what was the first thing they would want to do, they said that they would like to go to a mosque to pray.

Dr. Riffat Hassan, a professor of religious studies at the University of Louisville in Kentucky, is a trail blazer in the field of women's rights. She says, "*God who speaks through the Qur'an, is characterized by justice, and it is stated with the utmost clarity in the Qur'an that God can never be guilty of unfairness or tyranny....hence the Qur'an as God's word cannot be made the source of human injustice, and the injustice to which Muslim women have been subjected cannot be regarded as God-derived.*"

Constant exploitation of women in Islamic societies is not religious, but cultural. It stems from the huge chasm between the faith and our knowledge of the faith – between theory and practice. Abdolkarim Soroush, an Iranian scholar, has explained this phenomenon in his recent book, *Reason, Freedom and Democracy in Islam*, in which he explains why the religious knowledge is anti-women and why most Muslims are opposed to the idea of rethinking their ideology. Soroush has been heavily criticized for suggesting a reform in religious knowledge and the re-interpretation of the Qur'anic principles of the equality of men and women. This criticism comes largely from the male elite because it means giving up the systems of male privilege. How many men, Muslim or non-Muslim, would be open to that?

This knowledge, if made available, would bring to light that around 700 A.D., about 100 years after the message of Islam was received, women's rights were set into place under Islamic law, called *Shari'a*. According to these laws, Muslim women were presented with rights to voting, prenuptial agreements and inheritance. They could have abortions up to the fourth month of pregnancy and birth control was permitted. Muslim women could participate in battle and keep their maiden names. They also had the right to keep their wages. In attaining rights, Muslim women were centuries ahead of Western women. It was only in 1929 that Canadian women were actually declared persons and women in Britain were not allowed by law to keep their earned wages till the twentieth century.

Judith Tucker is author of a book called *In the House of the Law*, which is a study of Islamic law in seventeenth and eighteenth-century Syria and Palestine. She writes about a period when Muslim legal thinkers gave considerable attention to women's roles in society. Tucker shows how *fatwas*, or legal opinions, greatly influenced these roles. She challenges prevailing views on Islam and gender, revealing Islamic law to have been

more fluid and flexible than previously thought. In her book, Tucker studies court records from Ottoman-Syria and concludes:
1. the *shari'a* courts were accessible and popular with women.
2. the courts took upon themselves the task of defending women's Islamic rights against the vagaries of custom. For example, they would insist on a woman's right to a share of an inheritance or her right to refuse a marriage proposal against her family's or community's desires.
3. obtaining a divorce was easy for women who could prove one of the following:
   a) physical abuse
   b) mental abuse
   c) sexual incompatibility
   d) the mistreatment of her family
   e) abandonment for a year's time

This same *shari'a* is now misapplied and misinterpreted to crack down harshly on women's rights, keeping male dominance alive and well. Ironically, discrimination and victimization of women also increased with British colonization of many parts of the current Islamic world. For example, Western institutions would not allow women to open bank accounts without a male's counter signature. Women's assets were frozen and they felt the deprivation of their rights. Social, political and economic reasons also added to the problem, but the Muslim religion became the excuse that men used to legitimize their crimes. What is truly at fault is a misguided, narrow interpretation of Islam designed to serve a rigid patriarchal system.

Professor Amina Wadud, assistant professor at the Department of Philosophy and Religious Studies at Virginia Commonwealth University, has taught at Harvard University and is the author of a controversial book entitled, *Qur'an and Woman*. The daughter of a Baptist preacher, Professor Wadud is an African American convert to Islam and explains that as a Western woman, she would never have accepted a faith that is unfair to women.

Qur'an and Woman is a unique look at the status of women in Islam - a more equal and just status. For 14 centuries, the Qur'an, the guiding book for Muslims, was interpreted solely by men. Everything was filtered through male intellect, even women's issues. So, for a long time, men have told Muslim women about being women. This has led to Western misconceptions about the roles and status of women in Islam, and has also set a poor record of human rights abuses in many Muslim countries.

Dr. Wadud talks about some Islamic practices that have continuously troubled feminists, outside observers and Muslims: issues relating to polygamy, inheritance, women's rights, unequal witnessing laws and other injunctions that seem to discriminate against women. However, a new and deeper look at the verses in the Qur'an pertaining to these injunctions, the context in which they were revealed, the spirit in which they were intended, plus grammar and language variances, do much to clear up these doubts and misunderstandings.

Dr. Wadud also addresses many issues that have emerged in the last two decades that were never imagined or addressed at the time of the revelation of Islam, for example, rape as a weapon in war.

Spiritual equality, responsibility and accountability for both men and women are well-developed themes in the Qur'an. Through the Qur'an, God says: *"I shall not lose sight of the labour of any of you who labours in my way, be it man or woman; each of you is equal to the other."* Spiritual equality between men and women in the sight of God is not limited to purely religious issues, but is the basis for equality in all temporal aspects of human endeavour. As human souls, both male and female are absolutely equal in their relationship with the Creator and as Muslims, both male and female need to cultivate the same virtues and perform the same Islamic rites.

The Islamic Sufis loved to tell stories about female saints and spiritual women, so much of the Islamic history of female spirituality is told in folklore. There is a touching legend of Lalla Mimunah in the Maghreb. She was a poor black slave who asked the captain of a boat to teach her the ritual prayer, but she could not remember the formula correctly. To learn it once more, she ran behind the departing boat, walking on the water. Her only prayer was: "Mimunah knows God and God knows Mimunah." She became a saint greatly venerated in North Africa.

Later in history, the feminine gender was used in many mystical odes as symbols of divine beauty and perfection. However, these stories and others like them are not easily found in the history of Islam as it exists today.

The concept of gender equality is best exemplified in the Qur'anic rendition of Adam and Eve. The Qur'an states that both sexes were deliberate and independent and there is no mention of Eve being created out of Adam's rib.

The Prophet of Islam remained concerned all of his life about the status and treatment of women because at the time of the revelation of the message of Islam, women were buried alive, treated as chattels and at one point, considered to be inhuman without a soul. In his last sermon, the Prophet clearly asked men to treat women with kindness as, due to economic conditions, men were responsible for the wellbeing of their women. The Qur'an says, "and they (women) have rights similar to those of men over them...treat them in a just manner."

The Prophet's first wife, Khadijah, was a successful business woman who was 22 years older than the Prophet. It was she who sent a proposal of marriage to him. His second wife, Lady Ayesha, led a war, riding into combat on a camel. It has been narrated that when the Prophet's daughter, Fatema, entered the room, the Prophet stood up in respect. Fatema was a mesmerizing public speaker and her sermons have been recorded. Also noteworthy is Rabia of Basra, the first mystic of Islam.

There is a widespread belief that in Islam, the female is hardly ever religiously addressed except through the mediation of a male, and as an addendum to him. In the Qur'an, however, it is clearly stated that Umm Musa (mother of Moses) received divine communication. Again, Maryam (Mary, mother of Jesus) is mentioned by name in the Qur'an and an entire chapter is named after her. For those who believe that a woman should not be a leader, the Qur'an refutes that notion by telling the story of Bilqis, the queen of Sheba, who was a ruler of an unconfirmed location, somewhere in Yemen. Bilqis is referred to as powerful, strong and possessing a magnificent throne. The story of Bilqis, as it unfolds in the Qur'an, reveals characteristics of an adept politician and diplomat, who would be in her element ruling any country today.

In political life, there have been no less than 40 Muslim female heads of state. Fifteen of them were formal sultanas or queens who had the *khutba* (Friday sermon) pronounced in their names and whose insignia was minted on coins. In 1236, sultana Radiyya came to power in Delhi and 14 years later, Shajarat al-Durr mounted the throne in Cairo. On Radiyya's coins were stamped the following words: Pillar of women, Queen of the times - Sultana Radiyya bint Shams al-din Iltutmish.

In recent times, both Pakistan and Bangladesh have elected Muslim women as their prime ministers.

Gender justice is an important issue facing the Muslim world today. The lives of women have been comprehensively adversely affected by religious interpretations. While the Qur'an makes note of physical differences between men and women across time and culture, the division of labour between both sexes has exhibited some variations. Sometimes, what men do in one culture is done by women in another society. Their roles are seen as complementary and not competitive.

In the present time, the critical element Muslim women need is freedom to educate themselves to bring about change. Last year, the United Nations Development Program released the Arab Human Development Report, produced by 25 courageous economists and sociologists who asked leading questions, such as, "Why is it that there is such a huge illiteracy rate among women in the Arab world?" The conclusion was simple: Because of a deficit of freedom, a deficit of women's empowerment and a deficit of modern education.

The current dilemma of Muslim women is best exemplified through the words of Ali Shari'ati, a scholar and outspoken proponent of women's rights:

"Women who endure their traditional mould have no problem, and women who accept their new, imported mould have the problem solved for them. In between these two types of "moulded" women, there are those who can neither tolerate the inherited mould nor can surrender to the imposed new one: what should they do? These women want to choose for themselves, want to make themselves; they need a model; an ideal type. For them the question is how to become."

TO CHANGE THE IMAGE OF MUSLIMS, LET'S BEGIN WITH THE WOMEN
December 2003

My cousin visiting from France told me of an interesting incident. While studying for her master's degree in international business at Ecole Nationale Des Ponts et Chaussees in Paris last year, the professor in her organizational management class got an advance profile of all students. On the first day in class, he called her name and asked her to stand up and recite Einstein's theory of relativity. Although she thought it strangely irrelevant to the MBA class, she had studied physics, so she answered the question promptly and correctly. She told me there was absolute silence while the professor's jaw dropped. He blurted out, "But according to your profile, you aren't supposed to know the answer to that question!"

The profile outlined Amber as a 25-year-old Pakistani, Muslim girl who, according to his preconceived notion, obviously wasn't supposed to be knowledgeable about science. "Of course," said Amber with glee, "the professor apologized and the class looked at me with new respect after that - especially the guys".

Muslims, and particularly Muslim women, are fighting the image war at every level. Earlier in March this year, while the world was celebrating International Women's Day, I was battling a series of questions from a journalist about how I could profess to be Muslim and a feminist! To her, this was contradictory and in order to answer her query satisfactorily, I had to go through practically the entire history of Islam and explain a simple fact that many people forget, even when they study Islam: Islam was sent as a system of social justice and to free women from female infanticide, slavery, oppression and bondage. I also explained that, to me, feminism is about equal rights. In theory Islam gives women the basic rights to live, work, marry, vote, have freedom and justice based on the Qur'an. How these rights are being practiced today in culturally male-dominated societies is something the entire community must face and address.

Muslims in North America are addressing the issue of negative stereotyping at various levels. A recent Islamic Society of North America conference in Toronto discussed strategies. The able guest speaker talked about "educating the public about the faith". This is an important step in helping the host community understand the issues faced by this fast growing group of Muslims who are now the second largest minority in North America.

I don't know if there was a keynote female speaker at the ISNA conference, but there were no quotes from any women reported. At a time when there are major issues facing Muslim women, they should be invited to be in the forefront of any discussion regarding the community at large.

For centuries, Muslim women have disadvantaged themselves by allowing others to define *their* rights and responsibilities, and interpret the Qur'an through a male-centric cultural lens. But visionary scholars say that every generation of Muslims has the right to interpret the foundational principles of Islam to solve their own problems.

Through a non-Muslim lens, Muslim women are constantly judged by the yardstick of how the Taliban abuse Afghan women or how the Saudis oppress their women and don't allow them to drive. These inhuman actions have no basis in Islam. In actual fact, Islam is nowhere on the mind of these men when they force their patriarchal and oppressive rules on the women. It's not about faith - it's about power. Unfortunately for our image, the Muslim community doesn't always practise what it preaches, so theory remains far removed from the practices, which in some cases, are questionable.

Recently at a lecture in Toronto, well-known Islamic scholar Dr. Sachedina spoke about family rights and mentioned something that came as news even to my somewhat liberated mind. He explained that in a family dispute, the woman's decision overrules the man (provided she is not pursuing an un-Islamic cause). He further explained that any person who dehumanizes another or digresses from justice and humanity is not a person of faith. This lecture, attended by many non-Muslims, was another small step in the direction of removing stereotypes and pre-conceived images.

We still have a long way to go. The Muslim community worldwide needs to practise more of what the faith preaches - and harshly criticize those regimes or individuals who stifle human rights and undermine human dignity. It will only be through example, especially in their treatment of women, that Muslims will reach the end of this long journey to liberate our image.

SILENT SHAME: WIFE ABUSE CROSSES ALL CULTURAL AND ETHNIC BOUNDARIES

August 1994

Gori is a petite, soft-spoken and gentle young woman. She has a black eye and bruises over most of her body, the result of repeated beatings by her husband.

Counsellors have advised her to separate or press charges. She has chosen to stay in her marriage.

"It would be considered shameful for me to leave since there is a social stigma attached to a wife leaving her husband, no matter what the reason," she says.

Mina desperately wanted release from her violent spouse of many years. She tried seeking legal help but her husband and his live-in family threatened excommunication from her family and community.

Mina was kept indoors forcefully until she agreed to overlook the issue. She is still being abused, while those close to her simply look the other way.

Gori and Mina (not their real names) are South Asian and living a daily nightmare of abuse and violence.

Their stories are not unique, for wife abuse crosses all cultural, linguistic and ethnic boundaries. But immigrant women often face added burdens and difficulties imposed by language barriers, social stigma and unfamiliarity with Canadian laws and rights.

Within the South Asian community, as an example, "fewer women are willing to seek professional help or counselling," says Aruna Papp, an independent counsellor for Scarborough. She adds that the majority of cases go unreported.

Often abuse victims are unaware and uninformed about where to reach out for help. Many suffer from language challenges. Their agony is compounded by simultaneously dealing with adjustment to a new country, climate and culture.

South Asians are generally private people and do not like to talk about their domestic problems. The family is their pride and joy and they will go to great extremes to keep the family name from being dishonoured.

Sometimes that means trying to sweep domestic problems under the rug and ignoring abuse and violence.

When South Asians, whose former homelands include India, Pakistan, Bangladesh, East Africa, Sri Lanka and the Caribbean, come to Canada, their social and cultural norms are distinctly different from those of the local population. Typically, religion dominates the social code of life. This poses a huge problem: how to differentiate between loyalty to their own faith or culture and loyalty to life within the boundaries of the law in Canada.

For example, in some countries it is not a criminal offence for husbands to beat their wives. And very rarely does a court case arise out of such an act of violence.

"Many South Asians are living in a time warp of 20 years ago," says Afroz Usman of Awakening Family Counselling and Mediation Services in Thornhill. "They have physically settled in Canada but have not come to terms with, or accepted, Canadian laws. When there is trouble on the domestic front, they are more willing to let the elders of the family solve the problem rather than seek legal help."

Usman, who has worked with abused women for over a decade and is a board member of the Women in Transition shelter, cites instances where men from South Asia have married South Asian Canadian women as a means of getting immigration into Canada and then dumped them.

"These women do not turn to the law for help, either because they are terrified of reprisals or because they are under threat of dishonour," says Usman.

The perpetrator of violence in the household is not always the partner, lover or spouse, but may be a relative of the partner, says Papp.

"My prime aim is to educate Asian women about the law and their rights in Canada," Usman says. "Once they are convinced they can live within the boundaries of their religion and culture, and still be free, they can move ahead with their lives."

In many cultures, women are generally brought up to think of men in the family as the lords and masters of their lives. They are programmed to accept their lives as decreed by fate and take whatever is doled out to them.

But the scenario is slowly changing. Papp started the Toronto Asian Community Centre in 1981 and since then has set the ball rolling toward building organizations to help the South Asian community.

A victim of domestic abuse herself, Papp works with abused women and trains counsellors and caregivers. She has also made a video for counsellors on how to deal with spouse abuse.

"The needs of South Asian women are specific to the culture," she says. "Battered women will often refuse refuge in a shelter because it does not cater to their specific ethnic needs, like language, religion and dietary restrictions."

Papp explains that the South Asian diaspora is extremely diverse and that dozens of different languages are spoken in India alone.

"There is a burning need for more shelters aimed specifically at South Asians and catering to their needs," she says, adding there is also a lack of qualified ethnic caregivers in the community.

Leslie Brown, a barrister and lawyer, suggests that a simple awareness of Canadian law will grant women much needed security and protection.

"Cultural, social and religious beliefs are often the biggest barrier to getting justice," says Brown, who works closely with the South Asian community.

He has found that women will generally avoid speaking to a stranger about their domestic problems; others find language an obstacle, while many others simply accept violence as a way of life.

On the positive side, women with similar problems and from similar backgrounds are now forming into groups to help each other and train under professionals.

The interaction and knowledge that others, too, are suffering from the dilemma of domestic violence gives the victims, at least, moral support.

ONCE AGAIN

Once again I am
Battered
Beaten
Bullied
Brutalized
Once again because I am a woman;
Suppressed
Imprisoned
In the walls of my own making.
Once again I hear the words "sorry"
But they are empty
Bereft of feeling
Once again I am left on the edge
Of a precipice
Cold
Angry
Frustrated
Silenced
Once again I am powerless
Like all the other women I know
Black
White
Urban
Rural
Once again I want to cry out, run away
Once again I can't
Because the children are mine

MEMORIES ARE NOT ENOUGH
(a fictional story based on a true incident)
September 1994

My three-year-old daughter, Preeti, laughs as I chase her in the park. Suddenly she trips and starts crying, so I hug her. She wraps her tiny arms around my neck saying, "Pretty scared." (She always calls herself "Pretty"). As I hold her tight and tell her never to be scared, a vivid image flashes across my mind - the memory of a friend, the "other" Preeti.

I often wonder where and how she is. Maybe, someday, our paths will cross again. I picture her now as I saw her the first time, waiting for the subway at Kipling station in the place I consider my spot. I'm thinking, "She must be new, never seen her before." She climbs onto the same car and sits across from me. Usually, I try and catch a few winks but today I feel myself observing this striking young girl with interest.

She has beautiful, shiny black eyes lined with kohl. Set in a perfectly cut face, framed by auburn hair, she wears no makeup but looks exquisite. I notice she wears a nose ring like me and the palms of her hands are stained red with henna designs. When she moves her hands, her glass and gold bangles tinkle. "A new bride from my part of the world," I think to myself, jaded at the thought of how many years it's been since I was a bride sporting bangles and henna. She sees me looking and flashes a shy smile, probably noting that I have a similar "ethnic" look. I smile back and close my eyes to nap, feeling her eyes on me. But I refuse to be drawn into "idle TTC talk", as I call it. I have too much on my mind. My pregnancy is beginning to show, there's maternity leave to work out, and a decision on when to stop my volunteer work as an interpreter with the Toronto Hospital.

When I open my eyes, she's still looking at me, sort of sad and wistful. I chide myself for being aloof, but my stop arrives, so I ignore my inner voice.

Next day, she manages to find a seat next to me. She has such an engaging smile that I find myself responding so she says, "Hello," and hesitantly asks me if I speak Hindi. When I say yes, it is as though I turned on a light and instantly, I'm her friend.

In the next few days, my subway companion chatters non-stop and I listen. Her name is Preeti, "but almost everyone calls me "Pretty"," she says. She's been in Canada only a month and is learning English as a second language because she wants to work. Preeti informs me that her marriage was arranged through a matchmaker in her village in North India, a great honour for her family. Preeti said "yes" over the phone and after her papers were processed, came over to join her husband and his family. He's a taxi driver, and Preeti lives with him, his two brothers and their mother in Malton. Although I'm aghast that the practice of proxy marriage still exists, I don't say anything because Preeti seems quite happy. She has no friends or relatives in Canada and informs me that she was very lonely till she met me.

It becomes routine, five days a week, that Preeti waits for me at Kipling station. We sit together and chat till I get off at my station downtown to go to work and she continues to her classes in the East end. Preeti is like a curious child with no idea when to stop asking questions, but her innocence makes her invasions into my privacy acceptable. "Does your husband love you? How many children do you want? How much money does he give you?" Sometimes I answer, at other times I stay silent, letting her guess. Mostly I listen, because Preeti reminds me of my youth - fresh and passionate about issues, full of energy, while I'm weighed down by a difficult pregnancy, my full time work and mortgage payments.

In time, I start looking forward to my chats with Preeti on my one way trip to the city. (My husband picks me up to drive me home). I find her bright and articulate with a deep interest in everything around her and a passion for learning. Taking my cue from her personal questions, I once asked her how old she is, guessing about 20. She smiles mischievously, "On paper or truly?" and confesses, "I'm 16 but in my passport they've written 18." Seeing my slight frown, she laughs and says, "Oh, you're so proper, Mona - you've become Canadian and forgotten how we live back home. If they wrote my real age, people would have said it's a child marriage." Her spurts of wisdom baffle my mind.

As the months pass, I notice a change in Preeti. She's becoming pale, quiet and withdrawn. Once in a while, I notice burn marks on her arms; she says she burned herself while cooking. One day she says, "I miss my mother," and I suggest she call her. She replies in a low voice, "I can't - they won't let me." It's my first inkling that all is not well in Preeti's domestic life. I ask her if she's happy with her husband. Preeti thinks for a while and says pragmatically, "It's my duty to be happy - they paid a large amount for me." Seeing the shock on my face, she continues lightly, "You know my parents are very poor and we are eight children, so when his family offered to pay for all the expenses and some extra, my family accepted the offer. Mother told me that I have to do what they say, not only because of the money, but it's the honour of our family and if I do something bad, my sisters won't get married."

On the verge of telling her she's wrong, something about the intensity with which she believes this, makes me stop. I understand what she is saying because I'm a product of the same culture and consider myself fortunate to have beaten the system by marrying someone I love and who loves and respects me in return. But I'm apprehensive for Preeti, because I've seen similar cases of young girls being forced into marriages of convenience and mistreated. My volunteer work with the community has made me sensitive to the plight of South Asian women and the activist in me wants to investigate more, but I sense a pride in Preeti that holds me back. I make it a point to advise her of her rights, hoping things will work out for her.

One day as I get on the train, I notice Preeti is sitting in a corner looking out of the window, wearing a scarf wrapped tightly around her head. She doesn't turn to look at me and there's no response to my "Hi Preeti". I take her hand. It is ice cold. I ask if she's all right. Preeti turns slowly and my heart nearly stops to see that she has a black eye and one side of her face is bruised. Seeing my stricken look, she presses my hand so hard that it hurts and mumbles out of the corner of her bruised mouth, "Last night I got up to drink water and fell down." I know she's lying but her eyes are bright with unshed tears that say, "Don't ask me anymore," so I continue holding her hand and hope that some of my strength will transfer to her.

Preeti isn't on the train the next few days and I'm concerned. I don't have her last name or phone number to call. Recalling her bright laughing eyes when I first saw her, and how the laughter has faded away, bothers me and brings out the maternal instinct in me. Trying to find some solutions for Preeti, I ask the social worker at the hospital to get me some material on domestic violence and names of services where Preeti can turn for help.

A week later Preeti is at the train station again. Her bruises have faded but she still wears a scarf. I throw caution to the wind and give her a big hug. She's sort of listless and gives me a half smile. Suddenly our roles are reversed and I bombard her with questions. At first she doesn't respond but when I insist, she tells me that she is being abused by her husband and his family. "He accuses me of attracting other men with my looks and long hair and when I said I don't, he hit me and forcibly chopped off my hair. I cried out to his mother and she also slapped me and said I deserve whatever he doles out to me."

The picture Preeti gives me of her home environment is horrifying, but one I've heard before. Her husband works long hours, doesn't make much money and drowns his frustrations in alcohol. His mother and brothers are emotionally and physically abusive with Preeti and she feels they only brought her over to be an unpaid maid to all of them. Preeti tries very hard to please, desperate to be loved, but her husband is insanely jealous of her looks and is constantly trying to disfigure her face. Her sole outing and escape is the ESL class which she is allowed to attend only so she can perfect her English, find work and bring home money. I give Preeti the names of the organizations she can call for help and she looks at me as though I'm crazy. "I can't complain to anyone - they'll kill me or worse still, they'll send me back, which will hurt my parents. It's probably all my fault anyway".

"No", I say vehemently to Preeti, "it's not your fault but you have to get help before they hurt you more. I've see cases like yours before and I've studied the pattern. Abusive people don't change, you *have* to get away, Preeti." She looks at me sadly and says, "Mona, in your world you can think of getting away. I have no where to go."

"You can come to my house," I blurt out. Preeti shakes her head, "Mona, thank you. You've been like a friend and sister to me and just talking to you makes me feel better but this is my fate. I hope you don't have a daughter because she'll never be able to do what *she* wants in her life."

Preeti is not on the train over the next few weeks and I'm scared for her. A few more weeks go by and everyday when I board the train, I say a prayer for Preeti. I'm doing my last month of volunteer work at the hospital before my pregnancy makes me too heavy to do extra work. One day, the social worker tells me a very sick patient needs an interpreter. I'm staggered to see that the patient is Preeti. Her poor face is battered beyond recognition, tubes running into her body, she's on intravenous. I feel sick and have to sit down. After cajoling the nurse for information, I find that Preeti has internal bleeding and damage plus multiple burn wounds. Preeti slips in and out of consciousness. I take the day off and sit by her side. At one point, she opens her eyes and sees me - she acknowledges with a slight smile but her eyes are full of tears. Hospital personnel say she refuses to speak to them, which is why they called me, thinking she can't understand English. She was brought in by her brother-in-law who explained that she got dizzy while cooking, burned herself on the stove and fell down.

"Likely story," I fume.

I'm alarmed at Preeti's condition. I gently touch her brow and whisper to her, "It's all right Preeti, I'm here, no one will harm you now". At this point I've made a decision that I'm going to take Preeti away from the horror she faces daily. I don't know how I'm going to do it, but I will. I meet the doctor, social worker and nurses and tell them all I know. They are sympathetic but need a statement from Preeti before any charges can be laid.

My husband is concerned that I'm letting this affect my baby and he wants me to butt out. I can't - I'm her only chance. I tell him that I've offered to bring Preeti home and he accepts that helping Preeti has become my mission in life.

Next day, I'm at the hospital bright and early. Preeti is conscious and I speak to her at length about pressing charges, about women's rights and women's shelters. Preeti listens quietly. When I finish, she takes my hand and says faintly, "I was willing to accept anything, he could hit me and abuse me because he's my husband. I only fought back when his brother came to my room, drunk, one night last week and said that since the family had all pooled money to pay for my trip to Canada, I owed him a good time. I freaked out and yelled for their mother but she chose not to hear me. I screamed and fought, my husband came home and they told him it was my fault. So in the end they all beat me. I can't share this burden with anyone else because it's so degrading. I trust you, Mona. Promise you won't tell anyone."

With a heavy heart I promise, on the condition that she'll come home with me until she can face them again. She accepts in a resigned manner. When I come home that evening, I start having acute cramps and am confined to bed rest for a week. I call Preeti at the hospital everyday and advise her to wait for me, not to leave with her family. "Don't worry about me, I'll survive. You get well, Mona," she says weakly. "You have to be strong for the baby."

As soon as I'm up, I go to the hospital. Preeti is gone. They tell me she insisted that her injuries were due to an accident and she burned herself on the stove, so no one could do anything when her husband came to take her home. I wheedle the address from my nurse friend and take a taxi to the apartment in Malton. The building superintendent tells me the family moved out two days ago - no forwarding address.

Preeti's disappearance causes me great guilt for what I could have done. When my daughter is born, I name her Preeti in honour of my short-lived friendship with a wonderful human being. I plan to teach my daughter how to fight injustice and to achieve whatever she wants in her life.

MATCHMAKER IN THE SOUTH ASIAN COMMUNITY
June 1996

We're sitting in a quiet corner of an exclusive restaurant in downtown Toronto. I chose this location so we can remain inconspicuous. The two young people with me shall be called Vijay and Tanya.

Tanya, 19, fiddles with her handbag and tries to look confident. Vijay, 24, twirls his empty water glass, clears his throat for the umpteenth time, trying very hard to be suave. I try to blend into the woodwork.

With the three of us, there is no question that I'm the crowd. I am their matchmaker.

This is Vijay's and Tanya's second meeting, and their first meeting alone (if you don't count me). They met earlier at my house when the two families came together because they had indicated an interest in finding a suitable match for their offspring.

I set up that first meeting. The two families had never met; when they did, they liked each other. More importantly, Vijay and Tanya wanted to "get to know each other more."

And so, here we are on this chaperoned rendezvous.

I excuse myself to get some fresh air. The young couple looks relieved. I give them about half an hour alone. When I return, there's a little more animation on both faces, some laughter (a good sign). All's well for tonight.

As Tanya discreetly leaves for a minute, Vijay comments, "She's lovely, but I'd like to see more of her." I promise to try.

On the way home, Tanya indicates she likes Vijay. I breathe a sigh of relief.

Now the matter is out of my hands. Both families will follow up. If the match works out, I'll probably get a special invitation to the wedding. If not, we'll try somewhere else.

This, roughly, is the typical progression of an "arranged" marriage. Nothing bizarre about it. In the South Asian community, the custom thrives because the union of a man and woman is more than a marriage of two people; it is the confluence of two families. Simply put, in our community, family is everything.

And so that's my volunteer job: I'm one of those who help to bring families together. But I do this only with people I know.

Matchmaking is quite the scene in Canada because the social structure of the South Asian community here is not conducive to the automatic matchmaking that occurs in Southeast Asia. There, marriages are the natural outcome of continuous interaction among relatives, friends and acquaintances - plus the discreet help of meddling matchmakers.

I consider myself a bit of a meddler, because I come from a generation of arranged marriages. I got involved in this interesting exercise for two reasons (neither of which involve my bank account). My mother was a compulsive matchmaker and always said, "It's for a good cause."

Second, I realize that South Asian families living in Canada don't have the luxury of built-in matchmaking. For them, it is important to "network" and also have venues where eligible young women and men can meet and interact within the norms laid out by their community or religion - whichever plays a stronger role in their lives. People who know people who have eligible children are always interested in meeting other such people.

Besides, I have a vested interest: when my two boys come of age, I hope someone will return the favour.

There are some unwritten ground rules involved in matchmaking. If the two parties don't jive for any particular reason, it's acceptable to draw back. Usually there are no hard feelings.

Many Westerners don't understand that. They confuse "arranged" marriages of today with forced marriages, which did occur in the past and may still occur in small segments of Asian societies.

There also used to be "totally arranged" marriages, like that of my sister who didn't see my brother-in-law until the day they got hitched. Thirty years later, she is happily married, but that type of union wouldn't fly with today's young South Asian descendants in Canada.

The "semi-arranged" match is the one most acceptable to young and old. This is when it is set up for young people to meet and get to know each other, the families approve and the match is made.

The first time I arranged a match, it was for my brother-in-law, Ahsan. I was visiting England, he was in Pakistan and I got a message that there was an "eligible" young woman from a very respectable family in London. Would I please visit, show a photo of the prospective groom and check out the family?

I freaked. I didn't know what to do, how to behave, what to wear. But I made contact and was invited for tea.

Dressed in my Sunday best, I arrived at the house and was greeted warmly by the young woman's family. They served me an elaborate tea (this was the fun part) and we talked. I met Shanni (the prospective bride) and was immediately impressed to note that although she knew I was there to "see" her, she wasn't coy. She turned out to be incredibly sweet, well-educated and possessed of a great sense of humour (one of my personal prerequisites).

I knew my brother-in-law well enough to realize they would get along together. I showed her his picture and she said, "He's cute."

I figured, "This is easy," and reported back to my mother-in-law that all was well and they could set the wedding date.

What I didn't know then and learned fast is that members of the young woman's family have the right to make their own detailed inquiries about the young man, because they are, in effect, handing their child to a stranger.

(The young man's family may also make inquiries, but only with sensitivity. It is considered very bad form to in any way suggest that a woman is less than a suitable mate. The fear is that word might spread and dim her marital chances should this match not be made.)

In my brother-in-law's case, he was called by Shanni's uncle and grilled to the core. Despite being a smart, personable young banker, he was sweating and wanting to run away by the time he was halfway through the "interview". But the uncle was just performing his duty as guardian of the family.

While all this was happening, I waited it out in London and, finally, upon the uncle's approval, took the marriage proposal. It was accepted. Ahsan and Shanni were encouraged to write and speak frequently to each other on the phone (never mind the phone bills).

Six months later they were formally engaged; in another six months, they got married. Today they are happily settled in London, with three kids.

I don't always meet success in my attempts to match people. There was the time recently when I thought two young people were perfectly suited but, when they met, they couldn't stand each other. Before it became embarrassing to all of us, they said, "Thanks but no thanks." Without a ruffled feather, we all went our way looking for other prospects.

Success of a marriage, any marriage, depends on many factors, the least of them being how the couple met. To South Asians, marriage is a life-long bond of pride and honour, for the couple and the two families involved. If differences arise, the family will help patch them up.

A factor that may lead to the success of many arranged marriages is the expectation factor. Children are told that parents know best, marriage is forever and love after marriage lasts longer than instant puppy love.

Take the case of Usman, 26, who is a brilliant, good-looking doctor with a bright career ahead of him. A perfect match for any young woman. Usman lives in Toronto, is totally liberated and modern, and yet he agreed to let his parents find him a mate.

His mother spent the past year trying to find a "suitable girl" (as we say in the South Asian vernacular) for Usman, but one didn't come along.

A month ago, Usman went to Pakistan for a short vacation and saw a young woman his aunt had arranged for him to meet. They liked each other instantly, met a few times; the respective families approved of the match. Usman's parents were in Toronto and left everything in the capable hands of the aunt. A week later, Usman got married. He is back now, beaming with happiness and faith that marriage is a great institution.

Even in a culture where family dominates, there are differing views of marriage. Anu, 17, is typical. She says that when she is ready to marry, she will accept a match her parents choose, as long as she meets the young man and gets to know him.

"Even if I meet and like a boy on my own, my family has to be part of the arrangement," Anu says. "I won't do anything without their blessing."

That would make her the third generation in her family to accept arranged marriage.

Her grandmother, Pushpa, who is 69, had a totally arranged marriage. Pushpa's daughter, Renu (Anu's mother), now 45, had a semi-arranged marriage.

Anu frowns upon the word arranged. "I'd rather call it an 'introduction'," she says.

Her brother Rahul, 19, is not too keen on the family involvement scene. "If I love someone, then it doesn't matter about her family. Of course, I'd like my family to approve, but it's my life and my choice. Arranged marriages are old-fashioned and restricted to the Asian community."

But are they? Not according to my Italian hairdresser, who is in her seventeenth year of a happy, arranged marriage. Not according to my Chinese friend who says arranged marriages are still popular. Nor my Portuguese colleague who wishes there were more matches being arranged. Nor my Greek neighbour who finds arranged marriages a great asset in her community.

Then there is Michelle, mother of three girls, a WASP (white Anglo Saxon protestant) Canadian. "Now that I know how the system works, I'd love for my daughters to have arranged matches," she says.

"So when do I register them with you?"

COVERING MY HEAD DOESN'T MAKE ME BRAIN DAMAGED!
July 1996

Such a to-do about a simple piece of head covering. The desire for anonymity is one of the reasons Muslim women cover their heads. The other reason is personal choice. That choice is under fire.

One morning, I start covering my head. I make a commitment to myself to wear it for one year.

My family is surprised but they support me implicitly. They know that for a Muslim woman, covering her head is not deviating from the norm, but rather the accepted thing to do.

My husband warns me not to be defensive and to wear it with pride, if I decide to carry it through.

My reason? A deep, spiritual longing to be visible as a Muslim woman and to position myself in solidarity with other Muslim women who are suffering a backlash due to their choice of dress. I want to know firsthand what discrimination and stereotyping is all about.

I come to work with my head covered. No comment. A week later, when colleagues notice that the head scarf has become a permanent fixture, some curious glances.

My boss walks by my desk, does a double-take and retraces his steps.

"Is this the new look?" he asks.

"Yes, it is."

He continues, "Is it due to spiritual reasons?"

I explain why I have decided to cover my head. He smiles encouragingly and says, "Good for you."

A female colleague comments, "It looks so oppressive." I suggest she use a less hackneyed term.

"Did I look oppressed when I didn't cover my head?" I ask.

"No," she replies.

"Maybe your perception is affected by my outward appearance."

She concedes the point but is still not convinced. I'm not about to defend the cause.

To those who are genuinely interested, I spend time explaining the cause. To others, I simply say that I've discovered a new defence against UV rays or that I turned bald overnight.

I find that people are more accepting of the look, once they understand the conviction behind it and the fact that the decision has not been forced on me.

At the subway, a woman pointedly moves a few feet away from me. I laugh and say, "I did take a shower this morning."

She smiles sheepishly, showing surprise that I can elucidate my point in passable English. I try not to take offence when an ignoramus refuses to sit next to me. All this is a learning experience.

I receive mixed reactions from friends and acquaintances. Some drop me like a hot brick. Others try to change my mind for me.

The closest and most sensible ones take a little time to realize that I am still me. I have not changed. Only my outward appearance has changed.

I arrive at a job interview in my headscarf. There are many contestants, but I get the job. My new colleagues accept me without comment. I'm totally at ease with myself and the world around me.

I try to remain socially active, so that I can gauge responses. I attend my children's school functions and one child asks my son, "Why does your mother wear an earring in her nose?"

The perception of a child who is fascinated by my nose ring and unconcerned about my head covering amuses me.

On a few occasions, I'm invited as a guest speaker on a panel. When the organizers see me for the first time, they look embarrassed. I inform them gently that my head covering does not make me brain damaged. They relent and apologize.

I realize that the ones who are critical and uncomfortable are the ones with inadequate knowledge about Muslim women.

Vacationing in Bermuda and standing at a street corner, I hear someone say, "Salaam Alaikum" (the Muslim greeting meaning "peace upon you"). From my head covering, two young native Bermudians have identified me as a fellow Muslim.

I feel goose pimples along my arms and a catch in my throat. I never thought that my visual identity would be a bonus in Bermuda. I am at peace.

LIFTING THE VEIL OF IGNORANCE: MUSLIM WOMEN ON RELIGION, IDENTITY AND WAY OF LIFE
August 1996

Yasmin Syed Fatimi loves the reaction when she tells people she's a fashion designer.

"There are two reactions. A few people come up to me and compliment me on my "exotic" look. Others assume that I design only scarves or headgear. It's a typical reaction when the public can't see beyond my covered head!

"As soon as they discover that I have a diploma from Milan, design fashions for Western women and speak four languages, their attitude changes to one of disbelief."

Fatimi, 30, isn't fazed by these responses, having grown up in Europe, where, she says, acceptance of Muslim women was a long time coming.

"My mother, a European, is not Muslim by birth but by choice. When she accepted Islam and started living in England in the early '60s, it was unusual for European women to show their conversion openly.

"Today, things are changing, as hundreds of British women accept Islam under no coercion."

Fatimi's experiences are not unusual for Muslim women, whose identity, image and status are often the subject of myth and misconception in the Western world.

"I draw strength from my identity as a Muslim woman," she says. "It hasn't always been easy, because negative images of Muslim women in the Western media have created preconceived notions and prejudices."

Fatimi was educated in England, studied fashion in Italy, started her career as a designer in Luxembourg and worked as a buyer in Germany. As a result of her travels throughout the Middle East and Europe, she speaks fluent German, Italian, English and Farsi.

"Canada is by far the most tolerant country I've lived in, but there are still some preconceptions about Muslim women which stem from ignorance," says Fatimi, who came here two years ago.

"I feel it's our duty to project the correct image by talking openly about our lives and not letting others speak for us.

"No matter how closely a non-Muslim studies our psyche, they can't go into the depths of our being and see how liberated we are mentally.

"Muslim women have the right to property and inheritance. They can propose marriage and ask for a divorce and they can keep their maiden name (like I have)," adds Fatimi, who lives in Thornhill with her husband.

Moreover, from earliest times under Islam, there were women who expressed their views about public issues, she says.

"How else can one translate freedom and liberation? If emancipation is gauged only by the way a woman dresses, then no importance is being given to her mind, which goes entirely against the dogma of women's rights everywhere."

Unlike Fatimi, Nuzhat Jafri grew up in Toronto at a time when there were fewer Muslims in Canada.

There were "traumas" associated with being a minority, she recalls.

"Our prohibitions tended to become a joke for our peers. Once it became clear to my friends that a restriction, like abstinence from alcohol, is really a matter of choice, they learned to respect my convictions. That's what all religions teach us - respect for each other's beliefs."

Jafri, a management consultant, observes that her religion "has never been an impediment to my achieving success.

"It's been nurturing, not restrictive."

She came to Canada from Pakistan with her family more than 30 years ago, completed her education and embarked on a successful career.

"It's a misnomer to generalize that Muslim women are repressed, ignorant, submissive housewives. That's a fine line between urban and rural life found in every country."

Jafri, who lives in Scarborough, talks about the future of her 13-year-old daughter.

"I'll instil the same values in my daughter that were taught to me. These values have been a guiding light and very liberating.

"I believe in equal rights and work towards promoting a woman's place in society - equally to that of a man, while accommodating their differences."

Muslim women, she states, are denied rights not by religion but by cultural and traditional limitations imposed by a male-oriented society.

"Women are oppressed everywhere and it's unfortunate that in the Islamic world, sometimes religion is used as a weapon...the inane idea, for example, that Muslim women are not allowed to drive, just because some sheik in Saudi Arabia said so. There's no such injunction in Islam.

"Muslim women can do anything within the boundaries of reason and logic without compromising their status as respectable members of society and without being forced."

For Barbara Siddiqui, being a Muslim was a conscious decision.

Born in Midland, Ontario into a family that is still strongly attached to the Christian church, she is often asked if she was obliged to accept Islam because she married a Muslim.

"My decision to become a Muslim was a personal, spiritual and intellectual one, arrived at after years of extensive reading, research and deep thought.

"In college, I majored in religions, so I knew that Muslims are allowed to marry Christians, but I accepted Islam by choice about 21 years ago, married a Muslim, have three kids and no regrets."

Siddiqui, 49, and vice-principal of Valleyfield Junior School in Etobicoke, often finds herself cast in the role of unofficial counsellor and adviser to both Muslims and non-Muslims about her faith.

When she meets someone for the first time, she says, they are intrigued by the combination of her first and last names.

When she battles queries about the status of women, "I simply quote the Qur'an." The holy book says "men and women have equal potential for spiritual and intellectual growth, and share moral and social responsibilities," she notes.

Siddiqui finds lack of knowledge about the religion leads to misunderstanding about the status of Muslim women.

"Once I invited my mother to come to the mosque and she said, "Your God won't let me in." I had to explain that we have the same God."

DEATH WITHOUT HONOUR FOR WOMEN
March 2002

Strangely, the most disturbing image on the screen is not one of violence but an ominous declaration by some Muslim men that killing women who dishonour the faith and the family is a matter of pride. Three hundred people sit horrified, watching *A Matter Of Honor*, an unflinching documentary on the practice of so-called honour killings of girls and young women by close male relatives in Pakistan. These women are killed or burned beyond recognition if they are suspected of immoral activities which could range from being seen with the wrong person, expressing a wish to marry someone they like or going out alone at night.

The camera pans on to Foqqia Bibi, only 16, who has 50 burns on her body. The only sounds she can make are groans of agony as she cries out in torment. Married against her will, her husband's family sprinkled her body with kerosene and set her alight. By the time the documentary was through being filmed, Foqqia Bibi was dead. No arrest was made.

The occasion was a fundraising dinner earlier this month at the Talim ul Islam Centre in Weston, Ontario to raise awareness and money for the International Network for the Rights of Female Victims of Violence in Pakistan.

The dinner, organized by Thornhill educator Ahmed Motiar, was supported by The Canadian Council of Muslim Women, International Development and Refugee Foundation, Muslim Chronicle and York Region Islamic Society. Motiar, 59, is pleased a large number of men attended the dinner. "Violence against women is not just a women's issue," he says. "It involves men, so awareness has to be raised within a larger framework."

The audience is primarily comprised of Muslims from diverse backgrounds but it also includes a few non-Muslims. This problem is not isolated in the Muslim world; it has a menacing international presence and needs to be addressed across the globe.

Events in Turkey, Jordan and Pakistan have come to the attention of Western media recently, so the public perception is that this is a Muslim issue. So-called honour killings are totally and unequivocally against all teachings of Islam. Therefore, we want to erase this misconception and express a universal message of support and solidarity for those working for the cause of violence against women.

The guest speaker, a professor of religious studies and humanities at the University of Louisville and founder of the network, is such a crusader. Riffat Hassan begins her address in a light vein. "I've read many books on the rights and roles of Muslim women but have never seen anything on the rights of Muslim men...does this mean they have none?"

Men look sheepish, women applaud. Hassan, who has been accused for blowing the issue of honour killings out of proportion, explains the importance of the history of her campaign: "If a train becomes derailed, you have to go to the start to see the reason why it got derailed and only then can you remedy the damage."

In February, 1999, ABC's Nightline aired *A Matter of Honor*. One guest commentator was Hassan, the other Asma Jehangir, president of the Pakistan Human Rights Commission. "Following the show, I received a large number of e-mails and faxes from concerned individuals," says Hassan. "Two important sentiments were expressed: a strong sense of outrage at the brutality against women, coupled with a keen desire to take action; and a concern that the documentary should not be interpreted so that Islam condones or justifies honour killings."

The day after the Nightline program, Hassan founded the International Network for the Rights of Female Victims of Violence in Pakistan as a non-profit organization, mandated primarily to create awareness, mobilize a lobby against honour killings and collect funds for building burn units in Pakistan. In less than four weeks, 300 people had joined and expressed their support.

But Hassan also faced resistance and criticism.

"Many Muslims reacted negatively to the documentary, calling it biased and anti-Islam. They said setting up INRFVVP would only fuel the Western media's propaganda against Islam and Muslims," Hassan says.

This reaction was repeated in Toronto before Hassan's visit. It fell upon Hassan to diffuse a volatile situation and counter the criticism with her knowledge and expertise in the field.

"To those who are in a state of denial, I wish to say that what is important in this context is that, regardless of the intentions of those who broadcast *A Matter of Honor*, the fact remains that female victims of violence shown in this film are real human beings, speak in their own voices, whose intense pain and agony we see with our own eyes.

"By denying, ignoring or obscuring the occurrence of these horrible crimes, ranging from having acid thrown in one's face to being set on fire to being physically mutilated to being murdered...one is neither taking the high moral ground or advancing the best interests of Pakistan."

Hassan stresses the importance of addressing the issue of honour killings and taking steps to bring the killers of innocent women to justice. "Most such murders are never reported. When they are, the police rarely prosecute the killers," she claims.

Ominously, Amnesty International recently reported that "the number of honour killings is on the rise as the perception of what constitutes honour widens. There are signs that honour killings will become the next major international women's issue."

Hassan is aware of the fine line that separates cultural practices from those deemed Islamic. For 25 years, this devout Muslim has analyzed the differences between normative Islam and how patriarchal cultures have interpreted it. She clearly differentiates between culture and faith and says honour killings are neither condoned by nor part of Islam.

"Islam is not the reason these women are bring killed," she says. "These killings are not happening because men are following Islam - rather the opposite. True Islam is very protective of women's rights. The Qur'an offers no religious or ethical justification for discriminating against women. If we were to construct a society on the true basis of Islam, men and women would be equal in the sight of God."

Hassan has written many papers and books on the subject. She says in order to understand the psyche of those who discriminate against women in Islam, it is necessary to study the religion in detail.

"Women are discriminated and victimized due to social, political and economic causes. But religion becomes the *raison d'etre* and men use Islam to legitimize their crimes. This is the reason this reality has to be dealt with, from within Islam."

It was her personal search to find a niche for herself that led Hassan, a native of Lahore, Pakistan to the study of Qur'an and *Hadith* 25 years ago. Several years after earning a Ph.D. in England in 1968, Hassan moved to United States to teach and research. A single mother, she worked as visiting lecturer and professor at Villanova University, the University of Pennsylvania and Oklahoma State University before being hired by the University of Louisville. In 1991, she was selected by the arts and sciences faculty as "A Woman of Achievement". Hassan has also lectured at Harvard.

In February this year, frustrated by lack of action in Pakistan, Hassan wrote an open letter to the country's military ruler, General Pervez Musharraf, outlining her quest for justice for women.

There are some indications international pressure is working. In March, the government of Pakistan announced its opposition to honour killings and said it would improve medical care for female burn victims.

In addition, the first national Human Rights and Human Dignity conference was recently held in Islamabad. At the opening, General Musharraf condemned honour killings and said such actions have no place in religion or law. Honour killings, he promised, will now be treated as murders and medical facilities will be provided to the victims and their families.

"Despite such hopeful signs, much remains to be done," Hassan says. "Laws have to be put into place, support is needed for building and sustaining an international movement such as was launched for the elimination of female genital mutilation, and for setting up humanitarian assistance for the victims who are mostly poor and illiterate.

"Support is also needed for conducting investigative research so that hard data can be obtained for a systematic analysis of the growing problem."

MUSLIM SCHOLAR CALLS FOR REFORMS – WOMEN'S RIGHTS
November 2002

Khaled Abou El Fadl, often called "defender of the faith," has become one of the most powerful and controversial voices of moderate Islam in North America.

A regular presence in the North American media, the University of California law professor rarely speaks or writes without eliciting a strong reaction. His post-9/11 columns in major American newspapers were thought-provoking and critical of fellow Muslims.

Noted for his scholarly approach to Islam from a moral point of view, El Fadl stresses universal themes of humanity and morality, the notion of beauty as a moral value, and addresses the place of Muslim religious law in everyday life.

The latter is the challenge that poses problems for his adversaries. El Fadl believes Islamic jurisprudence is the heart of the Islamic faith but has been the victim of entrenched authoritarianism. He openly criticizes countries like Sudan and Pakistan, where many are calling for the restoration of Islamic law (*shari'a*), but where, he says, "assertion of *shari'a* is a political act which reduces women and minorities to second-class citizens."

Shari'a, according to El Fadl, "is a moral vision larger than any single set of injunctions or prohibitions."

Invited to Toronto recently as the keynote speaker for the twentieth anniversary celebration of the Canadian Council of Muslim women, El Fadl addressed the issue of reformation within Islam, focusing on women.

A world-renowned expert in Islamic law, El Fadl is a distinguished fellow at the UCLA School of Law, where he teaches immigration, human rights and international law. He has an undergraduate degree from Yale, where he was elected "Scholar of the House." El Fadl has a law degree from the University of Pennsylvania and a Ph.D. in Islamic law from Princeton.

"The love of knowledge is no different than love of God and necessitates originality of thought," says El Fadl, whose personal library exceeds 40,000 volumes on law, theology, literature, philosophy and history.

To hear him talk candidly and knowledgably about "dishonesty in discourse" within certain Muslim circles today is to appreciate his own courage of conviction and brutal honesty in exposing his less tolerant co-religionists.

"The Qur'an is a living text and inspires you to think," El Fadl explains. "It's a living, vibrant and inspirational text that engages in moral teaching by example - it's tolerant and egalitarian in its approach."

So where has the understanding and implementation of the Qur'an gone awry? El Fadl expounds: "The creativity and diversity of our faith as expressed in the Qur'an has been demonized by powers of despotism who suppress voices of reason..."

He refers to puritan Wahhabism, the strain of Islam that Osama bin Laden practises, in no uncertain terms: "We must take back our religion from the grip of those fascist-like patriarchs."

El Fadl, an intense person who drinks endless cans of Diet Coke, talks passionately about the crucial need to have coherent discourse.

"It's imperative to speak clearly, rigorously and truthfully to testify about our contemporary problems, including the status of women."

The tradition of *shahadah* (testimony of faith) has been forgotten in the modern age, he points out. "There is a huge gap in the way we wield our religion and the way we handle life."

Critical of dogma and rigidity in faith, El Fadl's background gives him reason to say this with conviction: "I was once one of those puritan zealots myself."

Born in Kuwait in 1963 and growing up in Egypt, El Fadl was on the edge of becoming an ignorant extremist in his youth, a fate he narrowly escaped when he decided to pursue knowledge instead. He learned about "cultural symbolism and tools of intellectual stupefaction" at an early age. He ran up against "*Hadith* hurlers" whom he cites as one reason Islamic intellectual thought and discourse have been stifled.

"I'm happiest when my blood is boiling and my mind is racing," confesses El Fadl, who prides himself on asking questions about everything. The challenges he faced only spurred him on the journey to master both traditional and modern learning.

He readily gives credit to his mother for influencing his life and thought as a jurist and modern thinker. "She was my first teacher in Islamic law," he says.

Beginning in middle school and continuing through his undergraduate years, El Fadl studied Islamic law with distinguished scholars in Kuwait and Egypt, accumulating *ijazas* (certificates) that would qualify him as a *shaykh (a spiritual master and Islamic scholar)*. During this time he witnessed the influence of Wahhabi doctrines that denounced teaching subjects such as speculative philosophy or mysticism.

"Looking back at our history, there were 135 schools of law in the first century and a half of Islam, and this is what gives Islam so much of its cultural dynamism," he explains. "It was *Kalam* (Islamic inquiry) in the field of theological disputes that preserved the Greek works. Today, Wahhabis denounce *Kalam* as heresy so we are back in the dark ages of Islam."

It is this philosophy of El Fadl's, his persistent exposure of what he calls "the schizophrenia that has seeped into Islam," his denunciation of Wahhabism and self-appointed religious leaders that has led to the challenges and risks he faces today. He has received death threats from Muslim and non-Muslim fanatics alike and police warned him that "unknown and suspicious parties" were staking out his home.

"I have no choice but to speak the truth even at the risk of confrontation because this is not the Islam practiced by our Prophet. When Islam becomes associated with violence, we have to take a stand."

El Fadl has taken this stand with faith and conviction through his books, columns and media appearances. Sometimes called a male feminist, El Fadl has been known to encourage his wife, Grace, to lead him in prayer. His current book, *Speaking in God's Name - Islamic Law, Authority and Women* (Oneworld Press, Oxford, 2001), reviews the ethical foundations of the Islamic legal system. In it he argues there must be a reformation in Islam with emphasis on women's rights.

"There is a need to rethink the notion of gender," El Fadl says. Islamic jurists talked about women's rights long ago, "but we have been alienated from our religious tradition."

His book is also an exposé of how texts have been changed to suit political needs and how many books on Islamic law by female jurists have never been published.

To say that El Fadl is concerned about the current status of Muslims would be an understatement. He is extremely troubled about the rise of Wahhabi Islam in the U.S., mainly because its followers dismiss knowledge and reason as unimportant. His critics are harsh and stoop to personal attacks.

"It's a lonely road and I feel sad because the worst persecution I've faced is by so-called liberal Muslim organizations. Their leaders feel they might lose control so they fight at a base level," El Fadl says.

Flanked by his wife, a convert to Islam, and his 13-year-old son, Cherif, El Fadl says he finds hope and solace in his students, who have set up and monitor a web site dedicated to him (www.scholarofthehouse.com).

"What choice do I have but to keep fighting for truth and justice till the day I die?" queries El Fadl.

A solemn thought for one so young.

WEAVING A WEB OF PEACE
July 2003

It wasn't tourism that brought women of various faiths and nationalities to Ottawa last month. It was their passion for building bridges, not of concrete and steel, but bridges of understanding, harmony and peace.

More than 400 converged on Parliament Hill for a conference on Diversity and Islam – Bridging the Gaps, the first initiative of the Canadian branch of Women Engaging in Bridge Building. WEBB is "an initiative led by women for women the world over, with many bridges to be built - the first one being a bridge between Muslims and non-Muslims," explained the organization's founder and head, Dr. Riffat Hassan, a professor of religious studies at the University of Louisville, Kentucky. "I use the term "engaging" in our title to reflect that our development is active and ongoing."

David Kilgour, secretary of state (Asia Pacific), told the conference, "It's appropriate that this first major event by WEBB, as a new international organization, be held in Canada. We consider ourselves bridge builders. This event allows us to see the enormous spiritual, cultural and ethical strength of Islam."

A few weeks before the conference, Statistics Canada reported the number of Muslims in Canada had doubled in the past decade.

The idea for WEBB was born in Milan September, 2001, at a conference on "Women Leading Global Change". One attendee was Louise Kissane, a businesswoman from Italy.

"I attended a session by Riffat Hassan, titled, "Encountering the Future," where she talked about the true face of Islam, focusing on the events of September 11 and stressing the need for building bridges," recalled Kissane. "Hers was a message for women of the world and she was an inspiration to all of us. It was a unique moment in history and I knew I had met someone who had the ability to move the world forward."

The next day, a group of enthusiastic women asked Hassan to lead them in a bridge-building exercise. They pledged their support and WEBB was born. It has chapters in Canada, Germany, Italy, France, Britain and the United States.

Kissane became a key patron of WEBB. "I've lived all my adult life in a Latin country and wanted to help women in Italy be independent, stand up and to take pride in themselves," she said.

Laure Capelle, chair of WEBB France, regards WEBB as "a worldwide family, a web made of women (and like-minded men) willing to promote peace and justice with respect, love and compassion between people all over the world."

Alisha Lehman-Wansing, head of WEBB Germany, wants to realize WEBB's mission to build "a fraternity (or sisterhood) through a better understanding of each other's culture, religion and beliefs."

Some of WEBB's primary objectives evolved from work in which Hassan is already involved:

- Creating change for women through education and raising awareness
- Educating women about their rights according to their faith, with particular emphasis initially on Muslim women, to prevent honour killings, abuses of power and other crimes committed against women in the name of God
- Establishing a network for women to enable them to improve their economic conditions
- Giving a voice to marginalized women.

Nazreen Ali, president of WEBB Canada, explained why the organization kicked off with a conference on Islam.

"Recent global events have focused unprecedented attention on Islam, which is the faith of over 600,000 people in Canada," she said. "The opportunity now exists to foster understanding of Islam, the diversity of the Muslim world and contribution of Muslims to Canada and the world."

USING WEAPONS OF MASS INSTRUCTION
July 2004

"When I was crossing into Gaza, I was asked at the check post if I was carrying any weapons. I replied "Oh yes, my prayer books". - Mother Teresa of Calcutta.

When Reem Meshal addresses her favourite area of expertise, Muslim women, she receives both darts and laurels. Keynote speaker at a recent Forum for Learning event, her topic was: *Muslim Women – Myth and Reality, Past, Present and Future*. As Meshal explored questions of the origin and evolution of women's rights in the economic, marital, educational and political realm of Islam, plus the impact of modernity and the controversies it has generated in the tradition from the perspective of cultural relativity versus universal humanism, she saw astonishment on the faces of her audience.

"I see this all the time. Either because people come with preconceived notions about women in Islam or because they have difficulty with the origins, development and evolution of Islamic theological, philosophical and social thought...or understanding that the broad controversies that shape Islamic theology are outlined and linked to developments in the field of philosophy, law and mysticism." For Meshal this wisdom is armour. "Without knowledge it's easy to become disenchanted (especially as a Muslim woman), it's instrumental in helping me find a niche and claim my intellectual and spiritual heritage," she explains.

As a lecturer at University of Toronto teaching Introduction to Islam for the past three years, Meshal tries to pass on that "intellectual heritage" despite the challenges she faces as a Muslim woman. "I get different reactions," laughs Meshal, 34, who has an eclectic group of students, some older than she is. "The non-Muslim students look relieved that I'm "normal" and there are mixed reactions from the Muslim students. Some expect a man or at least a middle aged woman covered in traditional garb!" She recalls how some male Muslim students gasped audibly when she first walked into class.

This doesn't faze her because teaching is a passion and she is well respected for her knowledge. "Some students take this course expecting an easy "A" because they're Muslim, and think they know it all. That's the first hurdle they have to overcome – that I'm not going to give instruction on how to practise their faith, but to teach them about art and architecture, law and philosophy, education and history. So while they're surprised, once they settle in and begin to learn, they're insatiable."

One of her Muslim students said "I love this class because we can't ask these questions at home."

Born in Cairo to parents who she says "were culturally conservative but religiously liberal," Meshal was always interested in acquiring knowledge. She studied in a Saudi Islamic School till she was 16 and learned at an early age that "it was mechanical education and there was no depth so I had to expand my horizon." She joined the American University at Cairo where she pursued Political Science and International Development. At 18, Meshal came with her family to settle in Halifax, where she completed her bachelor degree from Dalhousie University. "These disciplines still didn't satisfy me because I had an avid interest in the Middle East, so I thought that a study of Islamic history will certainly give me a good grounding," she recalls.

In 1997 Meshal completed her masters degree in Islamic Studies from McGill University, which she says "was an eye opener and extremely important for me to understand both my faith and the Middle East in modern times." Soon after her M.A., Meshal got a teaching position at the Department of Religious Studies at McGill, lecturing on two courses: *Women in Judaism and Islam* and *Introduction to Western Religious Traditions: Judaism, Christianity and Islam*.

Meshal has also undertaken unusual research projects. "As a research assistant to Professor Nahla Abdo at Carleton University, I was commissioned to research the issue of monetary compensation for women who were victims of war crimes in the twentieth century under international law and United Nations conventions. The research was meant to bolster the claims of Palestinian refugee women seeking compensation for confiscation of their lands in 1948 as part of a UN initiative". Obviously, with work like this and her upcoming project titled *Veiled and Unveiled: Canadian Identities in Construct*, Meshal remains continuously in the eye of the storm.

What are some controversies she faces? "Homosexuality is always a hot button. One student last year said "they [homosexuals] should be shot as they were in the past." So I tell them that the majority of jurists from the three Sunni schools of law (Shaafi, Hannafi and Maliki) ignored homosexuality, refused to legislate on it or make it business of the state.

It's sad to see some youth are confused and don't always accept facts. They'll argue with me, "but Islam says...," and I inform them that Islam is not a monolith so I ask who said it? Where is it recorded? Which school of thought? And they're lost - because they've been ingrained in one school of thought at home and never taught to question or read."

Meshal understands where her students come from and helps them to see the light. "I tell my students that in theory there can be five correct answers to every question because there are five legal schools in Islam."

"In essence," she claims, "I teach my class about *deen* and *daulat*, i.e. state and religion. I present most of Islamic civilization but let the tradition speak for itself so they can form independent, informed opinions."

While teaching the origins of Islam, Meshal talked about the common ties with Judaism and Christianity and found that many Muslim students had no idea about the similarity of these traditions. "It's a challenge. I see students who come entrenched in stereotypes and prejudice about "the other" and then I see these dislodged as the class progresses...so it's a feeling of achievement."

Meshal believes that religious education on its own places people in a solitary tower, so the ideal is to combine it with secular education. "Take the misconception about Madrassahs," she claims with enthusiasm. "Few of my students know that the concept of the Western University, the idea of an educational institution like a campus, is based on the Madrassah model in Islam. I try to empower them to pursue knowledge as a tradition of their heritage. I tell them that by the seventh century, Muslims had founded the house of wisdom in Baghdad. It was the center of intellectual thought and a cumulative tradition of the Muslim world".

Meshal sets her own role model. She is currently completing her Ph.D. on the interplay between custom and formal Islamic Law and continues to work on women's issues.

JUSTICE IS GENDER EQUALITY
November 2004

"Neither the sun shall overtake the moon, nor night overtake the day - this is universal justice" - From the Qur'an as quoted by Professor Azizah al-Hibri

Adept at balancing her life as an American Muslim, Dr. Azizah al-Hibri is a woman who is equally comfortable in both skins. As a Muslim lawyer, it took perseverance, reflection and courage for her to find a niche in secular America. In a 1996 article she wrote in The Technical Law review, titled *On Being a Muslim Corporate Lawyer*, she said, "I respect both religion and business" and talks at length about how her Muslim values complement her work ethics and vice-versa.

Al-Hibri is professor at the T.C. Williams School of Law, University of Richmond. She is also founding editor of Hypatia, a journal of feminist philosophy. She is founder and president of KARAMAH: Muslim Women Lawyers for Human Rights. A Fulbright scholar, al-Hibri has written extensively on issues of Islam and democracy, Muslim women's rights and human rights in Islam. Most recently, she guest-edited a special volume on Islam by The Journal of Law and Religion.

In Canada as a guest of the Canadian Council of Muslim Women, al-Hibri addressed a variety of topics with emphasis on women. In her keynote address she touched on the current dilemma of persecution of Muslims and their civil liberties. "The Prophet of Islam said that one day Muslims will feel like they are holding a burning ember in their hands. This is what's happening to Muslims in the USA and it's only a preview of what might happen in Canada," said al-Hibri. "Our observation at KARAMAH is that Muslim women have been victimized in the USA; 9/11 affected Muslim family life as a whole, but many Muslim women were hit hard, and they are reluctant to talk about their experiences [due to fear]."

Speaking frankly about Muslim leadership in the U.S., al-Hibri said, "Muslim leaders have been naïve...they were caught unprepared and responded with a knee-jerk reaction which is inappropriate. They missed the importance of engaging in civil society...of building bridges and doing grass roots work."

She continued, "Many Muslims feel threatened by the west because they don't integrate or develop alliances with civil society and organizations."

Al-Hibri suggested one solution is for Muslims to engage in dialogue and debate. "Roll up your sleeves and get involved in the political arena, so you will have a say in the decision-making process." She also asked Muslims to send their *second* kid to law school. Why the second child? "I know the first one will always be a doctor or engineer," she laughed, "but seriously, it's very important for Muslims to become lawyers and Supreme Court judges."

Remarking on the general condition of Muslims, al-Hibri noted, "There is a rise of kingdoms and fall of democracies in the Muslim world. We have allowed rule of law to be replaced by rule of the kingdom."

Al-Hibri has traveled extensively throughout the Muslim world in support of Muslim women's rights and acted as a consultant to the Supreme Council for Family Affairs in Qatar in the development of that country's personal status code. She visited 13 Muslim countries and discussed with their religious, political and legal scholars, as well as women leaders, issues of importance to Muslim women. She suggested, "We need to ignore interpretations that are totally illogical and patriarchal, and offer solutions based in the Qur'an that are feminist in nature."

On being questioned about Islamic law, al-Hibri said, "U.S. law allows arbitration process which is binding. Some communities in the U.S. that have tried to establish *shari'a* courts to resolve conflicts, find there are usually two hurdles: lack of expertise and the pervasiveness of patriarchal cultural views among those with some expertise. These cultural views tend to influence their reading of the problem before them and their understanding of a proper solution."

Al-Hibri explained how she has tried to overcome this concern. "In cases of domestic disputes or divorce, the community needs to produce an expert witness (because the judge is not going to send his clerk to study fiqh [Islamic law]). We feel the "expert witness" must have women's interest at heart. Our organization (Karamah) provides this service."

Al-Hibri is also working on a book on the Islamic marriage contract to provide a scholarly treatise for professionals in the legal field in the U.S. to consult. She said, "There is no adequate reference at this time. This book should help Muslim men and women understand their marital rights better."

Talking about KARAMAH, al-Hibri said, "This organization is dedicated to the empowerment of women through education, research and advocacy. A key goal of KARAMAH is the mentoring and training of the next generation of Muslim women leaders because Muslim women need to take charge of their lives and responsibility for the religion. Western courts are not responsible for getting the correct information!"

During the summer of 2003, KARAMAH launched a uniquely designed Islamic studies course, with special emphasis on *shari'a*. The course was created to help prepare Muslim women leaders address community problems and issues relating to women from an Islamic legal perspective. KARAMAH recognizes these leaders have a duty to formulate appropriate responses to the challenges Muslim women around the country confront in their own communities.

The four-week intensive course provided an introduction to four key areas: the Qur'an, the *hadith* (reported statements of the Prophet Muhammad), the *Seerah* (the life of the Prophet Mohammed), and major Islamic scholarly writings. The course also included the laws, rights and obligations relating to marriage, divorce, sexual relations, domestic violence, inheritance, dispute mediation and the laws of war. The class consisted of 10 women from various professional and educational backgrounds.

Regarding women's role in society, al-Hibri pointed out, "Islamic law gives women liberty and latitude. It's no longer a matter of choice; male leaders have been dissipated. It's imperative for Muslim women to rise to the front lines and not repeat the same mistakes. Our leadership is to unite and not divide the community. The best leadership is based on conflict resolution and mediation; otherwise there will be no leaders in the next generation."

Clarifying that leadership is not about women's liberation or feminist trends but a need of the day, al-Hibri advised the community. "Put your egos, insecurities and personal problems aside and find those who have leadership qualities and send them for training," she said earnestly. "Fundamental notion in the Qur'an is that of justice, and justice is gender equality. We need to examine Islamic jurisprudence and distinguish between cultural and religious practices."

Al-Hibri is also a member of the Advisory Board of the Pluralism Project (Harvard University) and Religion and Ethics NewsWeekly (PBS). She has served on the Interfaith Alliance Foundation Board of Directors and has been a member of the Virginia State Advisory Committee to the United Sates Commission on Civil Rights and the Religious Task Force for the Prevention of Family Violence.

I AM WOMAN - CELEBRATE ME

From the ashes of Afghanistan
Where you bombed my home and trapped me in a tomb of dust
I am the woman who has risen up like the phoenix
Protected by my *burka* - which **you** see as a symbol of suppression
This tattered cloak - is my only protection
From the mortar and shells
That you gift to my land - as you turn it into a living hell
I shatter the bonds, reach out my hand and
Gather the wounded and weeping women of my nation,
Stepping over the blood of our children as I teach them to say "no more"
No more - will we be pawns in the games of political power
No longer will we cower
I'll find ways to alleviate our ignorance and build walls within which we can learn
I AM WOMAN - EDUCATE ME

I am the woman from a village in Pakistan
Where they threw acid in my face because their honour was at stake
Battered, bullied and bruised - I suffered great pain
But the damage they have done has only fired my resolve
To never let them make MY honour, THEIR gain
I forced the courts to hear my case and took others like me
Caught in the vicious circle of male violence and frenzy
In trying to dehumanize us
My disfigured face has empowered me;
The cries of my sisters have given me strength in my own strength
I won't be cowed down by cowardly acts
I have found my path and will never return to the fetters of slavery
I ask for no accolades for my bravery
I AM WOMAN - CELEBRATE ME

I am a mother from the Middle East
Step-by-step trying to build bridges of peace
Surrounded by bloody hell
Where every shell

GENDER JIHAD

Has the name of an innocent bystander
I am Christian, Muslim and Jew
I bleed the same as you
I am wife, sister, friend and daughter
But our lives are devoid of any laughter
When our children leave home,
We are uncertain
If they will ever return
I AM WOMAN - VALIDATE ME

I am a woman of the street where I am forced to sell my body
Part by part
To the highest bidder - like a commodity
To those masters of the flesh trade who don't know
That we are women - we have a heart
And a soul that is torn apart
When we are used and abused like pieces of flotsam
Set afloat on the sea of time with no end in sight
We are a statistic on the pages of **her-story**
Not for the unequal wages we were paid
Or fighting the laws that are man-made
But - for being the principal victims of AIDS
I AM WOMAN - DON'T HUMILIATE ME

I am the Muslim woman who came to this land
Many moons ago
I couldn't speak the language, I'd never seen snow
I was alone and afraid with nowhere to go
For help, for advice about my woes
They scoffed at my head-scarf, my faith
My accent and the colour of my skin -
I felt forsaken
Yet I weathered all this on my own
I cried but I survived - thankful to be alive
In this land of the free
But are we ever truly free?
Today I am a victim again - after the terror of 9/11
My windows shattered, my mosque desecrated

It's ironical - but I am told this turmoil is created
By the very people who wish to liberate me
I AM WOMAN - LIBERATE ME

Most of all I am a woman like the rest of you
Privileged for the chance to share in solidarity
As I build the courage to stand up and speak out
Against atrocities heaped upon us
Breaking the bonds of cultural and social fanaticism to forge
A special bond with my sisters
In breaking the silence, I reach out across barriers of
Race and religion - in the one cause that binds us together
Our feminine souls intertwined with the souls of 14 others
They were women - therefore they died
WE ARE WOMEN - COMMEMORATE US

- Presented at WOMANVOICE on December 6, 2004 to commemorate the International Day of Action for Violence Against Women and the 14 women murdered at the Ecole Polytechnic Institute in Montreal.

FROM THE RITUAL TO THE SPIRITUAL
April 2005

(Traditionally, Friday congregational prayer is lead by a male Imam and constitutes a two-part sermon given before the prayer. The first part of the sermon is spiritual and the second part is usually political or social)

At the rate poison darts are soaring towards me, one would think I led a chorus line and not an Islamic prayer! Yes indeed, the *fatwas* are flying (I already have one from a Saudi network based in the U.S., thank you!). The Muslim community of the Greater Toronto Area, even those who profess to be liberal, are doing what has become the norm - condemning without considering, labelling without listening and judging without justice.

Let me confess where all this began. About three weeks ago, when Tarek Fatah, founder of the Muslim Canadian Congress asked me if I would lead a mixed gender group in prayer, I said No! I wasn't ready to be part of media frenzy. Tarek and I have agreed to disagree on many points, but we have what I call "a dignity of difference" - a respectful exchange of ideas which is a characteristic abysmally lacking in some parts of the Muslim community.

My husband convinced me that it would be a natural progression from giving sermons in churches and praying in synagogues and temples to lead prayer for my own community.

I checked with a professor of religious studies who was an Imam in Toronto. He categorically said that nowhere in the Qur'an does it specify women can't lead prayer. Also, during the lifetime of Prophet Mohammad in the seventh century, when he preached his message to a purely male dominated society, he did not speak out for or against women leading prayer. As a matter of fact, the women at that time were businesswomen, theologians, mystics and also participated in war. I'm extremely impressed by these female role models.

The three men in my life (two sons and spouse) encouraged me to take this leap of faith. What more could I ask for? I've always believed that God has created us equal and spirituality is not dependent on gender. However, there are many people who are barred from places of worship;

there are women who have stopped going to the mosque because of being stuck near the bathrooms or kitchen due to their gender.

More importantly, all worship in Islam begins with a declaration of intent. My intention was not reactionary, not defiant and definitely not a show of militant feminism. It wasn't about a battle between progressive and conservative; it was about sharing some profound thoughts with my fellow Muslims and also to help other women find a safe space to worship.

April 20 was Earth Day. After moving the venue twice (because the so-called liberal and culturally progressive centres refused to have a woman lead prayer), a backyard in Toronto's Cabbage Town became the sanctuary. A motley crowd of about 40 people from as far as Oakville and Pickering came to join in this historical Friday prayer, among them an Imam, women in *hijab* and diverse Muslims from various backgrounds. There was no security guard posted at the door to check I.D., credentials or people's intentions since I don't believe that is our mission in life. I am only responsible for *my* conscience and answerable only to God. This event was also an attempt to break the domination of a few misguided bigots who try to reduce God to a policeman.

Although physically I led the prayer by standing in front and reading the sermon before the prayer, we were all bound by our united submission to God. I felt we were truly blessed. Why? Because these brave men and women who chose to stand behind me and pray empowered me with a responsibility that made my own prayer more poignant and meaningful. It allowed me to move away from the ritual to the spiritual and actually hear and understand myself better than I ever have. At the end of the prayer, some of the non-Muslim observers had tears in their eyes and were touched to the core. Some participants told me they had not prayed in years and were thrilled to come back into the fold.

As for the critics, let me try and understand where their problem lies. Our message was one of tolerance, peace, spiritual equality, compassion and love of Allah and His Prophet. Obviously, that is not the message coming out of some mosques that base their sermons on negating others.

While this is not the ultimate move for reclaiming our place in Islam, it's a fact that our faith is frozen in time. Dialogue and debate, also known as *ijtehad*, an important cornerstone of Islam, have been deemed unnecessary evils and stopped since the sixteenth century. So the hope is that events like this one will open the doors to that much needed discourse and put us on the path to enlightenment together as men and women in faith.

First Sermon:

Surah Nissa (the chapter on women) in the Qur'an begins with the following verse:
O mankind fear your Guardian Lord who created you from a single person, created out of it his mate and from them scattered like seeds countless men and women - fear Allah through whom you demand your mutual rights and be heedful of the wombs that bore you for Allah ever watches over you.

I believe from my heart and soul that Allah made us equal in creation and wanted all of us to have this equality that is denied to many women today. What we are doing today is not *re-inventing* our own tradition, rather following in the tradition, the *sunnah* of the prophet. And how auspicious is this occasion today, being the birth anniversary of our beloved Prophet who is a mercy for all humankind.

The Qur'an says in surah 2, "*Even as we have sent among you a messenger from among you who recites to you our communications and purifies you and teaches you the book and the wisdom and teaches you that which you did not know.*"

What many people don't know, for example, is that the early mosque was not only a place for prayer for women, but was a centre for many other activities as well. It functioned as the school, where people learned their religion, and the parliament, where the community discussed new laws and affairs of the state. It was also the courthouse, where judgments were passed, and the community center, where families met their friends and neighbours and held their celebrations. In short, it was the hub and centre of public life for the emerging Muslim nation and women were active participants. It's sad that today women have been delegated to the back benches of the mosques and therefore we have to find safe spaces.

I'm often asked where I get the strength of conviction that I'm doing the right thing. I'm *inspired* by the first woman of Islam, Khadija, also called mother of believers. It is said that her wealth could cover the grounds around the *Kaaba*, yet she donated her assets to build that small Muslim community which desperately needed her support. I'm *motivated* by Bibi Fatima who relayed the Prophet's sermons to the larger community. Tradition records that when she entered the room, the

Prophet stood up in respect. I draw *strength and courage* from Bibi Zainab, who shook the court of Yazid with her impassioned *khutba* after the tragedy of Karbala. So we see a woman building an empire through her financial status, a woman stabilizing that empire though her piety and a woman shaking an empire though her passion for truth and justice.

There are stories of strong women in the Qur'an, stories of Mary, mother of Jesus, Bilquis, the queen of Sheba and mother of Moses to name just a few. Later, a considerable number of women of the ninth and tenth centuries are mentioned in the Arabic and Persian sources for their extraordinary achievements in mysticism as well as being poets, calligraphers or jurists.

Today, I feel moved that we are gathered here to submit to Allah and pay tribute to His loving Prophet Mohammad. When we celebrate the Prophet's life, we celebrate the women of his family and the other women of Islam. Women who took their direction from him – a man who is a mercy for our hearts in allowing them to open up on truth in all aspects of life, and a mercy for our hearts, making them full of love for all people, and a mercy for our lives as we seek to establish justice in our relations. Prophet Mohammad taught us many things, but one important lesson is that the more you live the greatness of God in you, the more pious and God-loving you become. You would know the meaning of being a human being as well as how much every human being needs Allah and how all human beings are equal before him, with the most pious among them becoming the closest to Allah.

Second Sermon:

My friends, the greatest *jihad* - inner struggle - for us today, is the *jihad* to speak the truth. And speaking truthfully, irrespective of the consequences, means not condemning anyone or passing judgement on anyone for Allah has clearly said in the Qur'an:

Let there be no compulsion in religion: Truth stands out clear from error. Whoever rejects Shaitan and believes in Allah has grasped the most trustworthy handhold that never breaks. And Allah knows and hears all things.

Where we find ourselves short is the ability to speak the truth, even in front of an unjust ruler. Our easiest escape is to blame the West for all the ills of the East. We have to search our own souls and ask ourselves where in this holy book does it say that we have to be addressed every Friday by bigots, hypocrites, liars and give unholy allegiance to the despotic rulers we have today in the Muslim kingdoms? Where does it say that women can't drive? Forget leading prayers, most women can't even enter a mosque except by the kitchen. Where does it say to look down upon and humiliate people who don't conform to our way of thinking? We know where this comes from but as they say in Canada, we won't even go there. We'll concentrate on the fact that the Qur'an repeatedly reminds us that humanity is one community.

As an interfaith advocate, let me assure you that all is not doom and gloom. Each religion has its own problems to deal with and we should leave it to them to sort out, while we concentrate on ours. If we stop following the principal of *amal bil maroof - nahi anal munkir* - enjoin that which is good and condemn that which is wrong - we will always give others an excuse to usurp our lands, widow our women and orphan our children.

Today, it doesn't matter who leads prayers. This event is just to break the domination of a few misguided bigots who try to reduce God to a policeman and whose only interest in "profit" is the kind that comes out of their bank account.

So each one of us is empowered to take with us a message of peace, justice, equality, tolerance, compassion and open mindedness. This is not my message or that of our host - this is the message of the book!

PART 3

SPIRITUAL JIHAD -
A STRUGGLE TO KNOW EACH OTHER

"O people we have made you into nations and tribes
so that you may know one other"
The Qur'an

THE NEED FOR COMPASSION AND TOLERANCE
Sept 30, 2001

In the name of God, the most gracious, most merciful
Praise to God, the Cherisher and sustainer of the worlds
Most gracious, most merciful
Master of the of judgment
Is it you we worship, it is you we ask for help
Show us the straight way
The way of those on whom you have bestowed your grace - those whose portion is not wrath and those who do not go astray
(Al-Fateha - Qur'an)

This verse from the Qur'an is called the heart of the Qur'an. Many scholars believe that it encapsulates the entire spirit and essence of the holy book. It has also been likened to the Christian Lord's Prayer. We, as Muslims, recite this verse many times a day as we offer our five formal daily prayers and this prayer is a guide for us.

We begin by praising God and calling Him merciful and compassionate.

The understanding is that if we wish for God to be compassionate and merciful towards us, we must show the same compassion and mercy towards His creation - which is the people around us. This may sound like a cliché but I always explain that I respect those who are my brothers and sisters and faith and I embrace those who are my equals in creation.

The Qur'an emphasises the importance of human beings' vital relationships with God, his parents or the people around him in many verses. The Ten Commandments that Allah revealed to prophets Moses and Jesus constitute a complete guide that ensures the stability and safety of both the individual and society. Islam places great importance on social justice and ethical values.

We pray about mercy and accept that life and death are only in the hands of God. The Qur'an says: *"and slay not the life which Allah has made sacred, save in the course of justice."* God wants us to respect human life, telling us that killing one person is like killing all of humanity.

If we take this in context of the tragic events of September 11, which left thousands dead, hundreds physically injured and the rest of the world spiritually wounded, we must understand very clearly and without a shred of doubt that the people who perpetrated this ghastly crime were not people of God.

They were those who went astray and if they used the name of Islam for the acts they committed, then they hijacked our faith. There is a verse in the Qur'an that translates: *enjoin the good and condemn that which is evil or bad.*

We, as practicing Muslims, totally condemn any action of violence against innocent people. Islam teaches us to differentiate between right and wrong, between good and evil, between justice and injustice, between combatant and non-combatant, between legitimate and illegitimate use of force. There are no grey areas in our understanding of these terms. As Muslims, we have been given very clear parameters between what is right and wrong. The Qur'an says, "*the Islamic relationship between individuals and nations is one of peace....Muslims learn from the Qur'an that that God's objective in creating the human race in different communities was so that they could relate to each other peacefully.*"

However, the Qur'an also says that in some cases war becomes a contingency, especially as a means of self-defence. But even in such a case, there are extremely stringent rules of war. The Prophet of Islam told his companions and followers in the instance of the first war of Islam, when their lives were threatened and they had to revert to self-defence, that they could never harm innocent people, children, civilians, old people, people engaged in any worship or destroy crops and animals.

The Qur'an says, "*only the combatants are to be fought and no more harm should be caused to them then they have caused.*" Thus wars and weapons of destruction that destroy civilians and their towns are totally ruled out by the Qur'an and by practise of the Prophet. This brings us to the very interesting and unending debate about the word *jihad* - misused and misrepresented by a few wrongly guided people.

It's very clear in the Qur'an that there is no such thing as Holy war. In actual fact, fighting a global battle against terrorism becomes by default our *jihad* in the true sense because *jihad* means struggle of good over evil.

The Qur'an says further: "*war may become necessary only to stop evil from triumphing in a way that would corrupt the earth.*"

So what else is terrorism but evil? In accordance with our Islamic mandate, we can't let it triumph. Terrorism is an attack against innocent civilians irrespective of their faith; terrorism is murder and genocide; terrorism is inherently evil no matter where it's generated from. The analogy of terrorism is like that of cancer; it's a disease that needs to be rooted out from the base and its connected cells need to be destroyed, otherwise it will raise its ugly head again and again.

So let us try and bring some order into this disorderly mess through our faith communities. Our faith tells us that in every time of darkness, there is some light. It's unfortunate that it had to take a catastrophe like 9/11 to bring us together, but we should continue to pray together and we should try and empower others to turn to prayer.

This is our only salvation. Let's pray for those who need it.

Let's accept our emotions without letting them disable our clarity. Let's resolve to do what we can in our own humble way to help create a world of understanding, compassion, courage and most of all - love.

JESUS IN ISLAM
October 2001

Islam, the faith of 1.3 billion people across the globe today, is a continuation of the tradition of Abraham, therefore embracing the two traditions preceding it, Judaism and Christianity.

Moses and Jesus preceded Mohammad as prophets and messengers, bringing the message considered to be the word of God and recorded in the Torah, the Bible and then the Muslim's Qur'an. Therefore, Muslims look upon Jews and Christians as "people of the book."

In Islam, we revere Jesus as a prophet, whom Muslims believe was privileged by being given unique characteristics of healing by God, in a way that was never precedented or repeated, so that it could be proof of the existence of God and His great mercies to mankind.

The word *Muslim* means to "submit" to God. We believe that Jesus submitted to God in the most complete way through his compassion, justice and mercy for others. It's interesting that Jesus and his teachings are mentioned more times in the Qur'an, than Mohammad.

The references to Jesus in the Qur'an start with Mary. There is an entire chapter devoted to the birth of Jesus in the chapter titled *Maryam* (Mary). In this, God tells us about Jesus and his mother to inform us about his mortal and human nature. "*Christ, son of Mary, was a messenger like many of the messengers that passed before him. His mother was a woman of truth.*" (Qur'an). Jesus performed miracles by God's permission just as God empowered Moses and several other prophets with miracles. God elevated their spirituality and humanity.

The Qur'an says that Mary was a faithful believer in God and asked God to protect her from Satan. "*And her Lord accepted her with full acceptance and vouchsafed to her a goodly growth - prepared the conditions for that upbringing - and made Zakaria her guardian.*" And it is believed that the angels said, "*O Mary Lo God gives thee glad tidings of a word - and God's word is His will - from him whose name is Messiah, Jesus, son of Mary, illustrious in the world and the Hereafter, and one of those brought near to God.*" (Qur'an).

It was said that Jesus would speak to mankind in his cradle - a miracle to prove the falsehoods of all the accusations concerning that Mary had a child - and he would be one of the righteous. Jesus said: "*I am indeed a servant of Allah: He hath given me revelation and made me a prophet; And He* hath made me Blessed wherever I be and hath enjoined on me Prayer and Charity as long as I live; (He) hath made me kind to my mother and not overbearing or miserable; So Peace is on me the day I was born, the day that I die and the Day that I shall be raised up to life (again)!"

Regarding Jesus, the Qur'an says, "And he will teach him the scripture (the theory and the wisdom to learn how to put it into practise), and the Torah and the Gospel. And will make him a messenger unto the children of Israel." It is believed that Jesus explained he had a sign from God, a sign that had to do with healing in a way that was miraculous and had to do with his relationship to God directly and not dependent upon human abilities. Jesus said, "I fashion for you out of clay the likeness of a bird, and I breathe into it and it be a bird, by God (it is God that gives it life). I heal him who was born blind, and the leper, and I raise the dead, by God's leave. And I announce unto you what ye store in your houses. Lo, herein verily is a portent for you, if ye are believers." (Qur'an)

The Qur'an goes on to say, "Lo, the likeness of Jesus is as the likeness of Adam (both were created without a father). He created him of dust, then He said unto him, Be! And he is."

Muslims do not believe in the Trinity and have Jesus quoted as saying, "Lo I am a human being, not a God. Allah is my Lord and your Lord so worship Him. That is the straight path."

When Jesus became conscious of the disbelief of people about his prophet-hood, he cried, "Who will be my helpers in the cause of God?" The disciples said, "We will be God's helpers. We believe in God and bare thou witness that we surrendered unto Him."

And then God said, "O Jesus, Lo I am gathering thee and causing thee to ascend unto Me, and am cleansing thee of those who disbelieve and am setting those who follow thee above those who disbelieve until the day of Resurrection. Then unto Me ye will (all) return and I shall judge between you as to that wherein ye used to differ."

THE WHIRLING DERVISHES IN TORONTO
October 2001

A few years ago, when I was actively involved as a board member on Islamic Media Awareness Group, we produced a 13-part series for Vision Television called SALAAM. Salaam was generally very well received because our mandate was broad and the idea was to reflect Islam in its glory and diversity. During this time, the Whirling Dervishes visited Toronto for their annual performance and our producer did a small piece on the Dervishes, mentioning the fact that they are part of the Sufi Tradition in Islam. We received both positive and some negative feedback and since that time, it has been my desire to see for myself what this experience is all about.

So, when the Whirling Dervishes from Konya, Turkey performed at Massey Hall in Toronto, I went to see them. To say that it was an experience would be an understatement. I am not an active follower of the Sufi tradition, a way of life whereby religion is conceived at a singular level, each individual soul seeking and finding salvation. But I keep an open mind, believing that as long as the path leads to Allah, I am willing to follow it.

Massey Hall has seating for approximately 2,800 people and it was full. The attendees were not all Muslims. My guess is that 90 percent of them were non-Muslims. The program started with Surah Fateha (the opening verse of the Qur'an) recited by the Shaykh in a serene resonating voice. Not once did the ensemble compromise their principles by reverting to non-Muslim practices. They said *Salaam Alaikum* and gave a brief history of their tradition. The first half of the performance was by an orchestra that played unusual instruments, like the Ney flute. The vocals were a mixture of recitations and invocations in an amazingly striking tone by Kani Karaca, who is blind. In between, they recited salutations on the Prophet. This was followed by recitation from the Qur'an. All this was delivered in a language that the audience could not understand.

There was pin-drop silence in the hall. I saw a couple of people around me wipe away tears, they were so overwhelmed. I was, too. The chanting came from the heart and went straight to the heart. At intermission, the ensemble got a standing ovation.

During intermission, literature on Islam and Sufism was distributed. The literature contained translations from the Qur'an as well as lists of books and CDs on mainstream Islam. The books and tapes were sold out in the first 15 minutes.

The second half of the evening was devoted to the experience of whirling. The Shaykh explained that this tradition dates back seven centuries. Followers of the thirteenth century movement founder Jelaluddin Rumi, known as Mevlana, the Dervishes contribute to powerfully haunting episodes that describe the saga of a journey from life to death. The ritual involves a seven-segment procedure in which seven Dervishes launch into a series of whirls, each rotating on his own axis perhaps 1,500 times in 30 minutes, without a break. The Dervishes eyes are closed and they move with grace and fluidity, right hand slightly elevated in search of Allah's love and self-discovery. To the uninitiated, this could be extremely monotonous, but the audience was mesmerized. At the close of the performance they did not applaud but cried, *Bravo!*

I'm not in a position to stand in judgment about what is right or wrong with the performance of the Whirling Dervishes; all I can say is that it has been a long time since I saw such a positive event and response to Islam. At this time in history, when Muslims are fighting negative images, the Dervishes were like a breath of fresh air, especially in terms of reaching a non-Muslim crowd. We were all touched by the spirituality. I felt tears in my eyes and I saw the looks on the faces of people around me.

A Toronto Star critic who covered the event was rather sceptical in his review, but he ended his piece with these words: "If the churches of the West had such distinctive ambassadors, then perhaps their pews would be full again."

PURSUING PEACE THROUGH EDUCATION AND KNOWLEDGE
March 2002

At a point in the history of the world, when religious intolerance is at an all time high, it's rare and refreshing to find a religious scholar who actively and consistently promotes peace and harmony. Dr. Abdulaziz Sachedina cherishes inclusiveness of all faiths. "The more I study other faiths, new traditions and various schools of thought, the more I understand my own faith," says Sachedina.

Professor of Religious Studies at University of Virginia, he is a recognized expert in Islamic theology, law and ethics in the U.S. He sits with the U.S. congress and senate on a range of issues from cloning to biological research and is available to give advice on Muslim matters such as dietary laws in prison to wearing a beard in the police force. Apart from academia, Sachedina is an icon among Muslims of North America for his work in bringing the community together.

Sachedina's love for learning and imparting knowledge stems from his childhood. Born in Tanzania where he completed high school in Dar-es-Salaam, he says, "Although my father died when I was 12, I recall growing up in an atmosphere that was scholarly and intellectual, where reading was a tradition. I was drawn to a study of religion, and had a penchant for teaching and lecturing at a young age." Influenced strongly by his mother, Sachedina says, "My mother was a teacher, public speaker and advocate for women's rights and following her footsteps, I taught math, English and religion at age 13 to children younger than I." Well on his way to becoming the powerful orator he is now, at age 17 Sachedina had his first experience in public speaking when he addressed over a thousand people about the Prophet of Islam and his teachings. He was a confident young man - too confident, he explains. "Along with the religious influences I also inherited certain unhelpful attitudes - a defensiveness and narrow view of human religiosity so I used to argue about religion constantly when I was a youth."

All this changed in 1967 when Sachedina went to Iran take his B.A. Honours in Persian language and literature. In Iran, he also took private lessons to learn Arabic and Islamic Sciences, including law, jurisprudence, theology, tradition and history. "One of the greatest influences in my life and work is that of my teacher, Dr. Ali Shari'ati, well-known sociologist, historian and philosopher. Dr. Shari'ati saw history as an instrument of recording human experience as it goes through self-development and my analysis of history is influenced by his teachings. Dr. Shari'ati taught us to look at history as a whole, about inclusiveness and how to strengthen religious knowledge without sectarianism."

Commenting on religious violence, Sachedina laments, "I'm extremely saddened by people fighting in the name of religion. We can't use history to relive our differences. We need to use history to move on and resolve those differences through dialogue - not to make the same mistakes. And dialogue is between equals. We have no right to control the showering of divine mercy on humanity."

Sachedina's immense passion for peace shows on the contours of his face and the sadness in his eyes when he talks about sectarian violence. "Religion becomes a weakness when used for violence by self-righteous and ignorant people and ignorance can only be erased through reading and reflection."

In his fervent pursuit of peace and understanding between communities, Sachedina cites a quotation from the Qur'an which he used as an introduction to a recent series of lectures. *"...and had God not checked the evil oppressors among the people....a great number of monasteries, churches, synagogues and mosques where God's names is mentioned frequently would have been by now destroyed."* Attended largely by Muslim youth and non-Muslims, the purpose of these lectures was to remove barriers and bring people together. Sachedina moves easily from Arabic to Persian and back to English, equally comfortable in Swahili, Gujrati, Urdu, Hindi, French or German.

Author of numerous books and papers, Sachedina, 58, has a soft spot for Toronto. "I share a special connection with Toronto for many reasons," he says. He proves this by coming to Toronto whenever he can, to share his knowledge and findings. From 1971 to 1976, Sachedina was a student at the University of Toronto where he completed his Master's degree and Ph.D. in Islamic and Middle Eastern Studies. "Toronto was my first stint at studying Islam in the West and it was an eye opener. My teachers constantly challenged me to look in from the outside. I had already studied Islam from a religious perspective but Toronto was an opportunity to study Islam from a historical and intellectual perspective, a methodology which forced me to be objective." He smiles as he recalls,

"When I presented my first dissertation proposal, my professor threw it back at me calling it defensive and subjective. Fact is, I *was* defensive about my faith and I'm grateful to my professors who forced me to weigh the strengths and weaknesses of my own belief system, as an outsider."

Sachedina doesn't downplay the effort his U of T professors to take him through this journey without hurting his faith. "It was a transition from believer to observer and it helped me see the beauty of Islam as an outsider. Contours and landscape are always sharper and more attractive from a distance."

Sachedina's first job in 1976 was teaching Islam in Ontario at the University of Waterloo and Wilfred Laurier University. "This was a time when Islamic history was a relative stranger to North American culture. It was considered history of "the other." The approach was patronizing and the methodology, orientalist, but thanks to my professors, I was prepared for the challenges."

In forty years of teaching at various academic institutions all over the world and lecturing his own community, Sachedina stresses the importance of reading and research. "Our community in general is not a reading community. We tend to read only that with which we agree and have a comfort level, not anything that makes us think. This is detrimental to religion."

The Muslim community, which like many others, is victim of sectarianism, is not wholly comfortable with Sachedina's push for unity and minimizing differences. And Sachedina has been hurt by the implications. "The community has difficulty choosing between academic language and the emotional rhetoric of the mosque. But I am an academic and have a responsibility towards history and to the community. In Islam, there is freedom to develop scholarship freely and this means that there is something to be learned from all scholarly works - irrespective of faith or sectarian leanings."

Do the challenges ever deter him? "I believe in the power of divine guidance. When you enjoy what you do, you find a spiritual reward. I'm exhilarated when I read books, learn something new, or write a paper and I believe that from the Islamic perspective, if I stay within the sphere of what the Qur'an teaches, I'm blessed."

He talks animatedly about his three current challenges. "I'm working on a web site course on the mystical dimension of Islamic tradition which deals with Islamic art and architecture as an expression of Islamic

Spirituality. I'm also working on a project on Islamic law for Muslim physicians, which undertakes to investigate judicial rulings in the section of Islamic law that deals with issues of bioethics.

Another project is a comparative study of legal methodology in Islamic schools of legal thought. Sachedina is examining the work of Muslim jurists from five schools of Islamic law, four Sunni and one Shiite.

Sachedina sits on more than a dozen advisory and editorial boards, including the Encyclopedia of Ethics, Oxford Dictionary of Islam, Center for Strategic and International Studies, Journal of American Academy of Religion and Tanenbaum Center for Interreligious Understanding.

BUILDING RELIGIOUS INCLUSIVITY IN ONTARIO
March 2003

An address was delivered to a multi-faith audience at Queen's Park, Toronto

Building religious inclusivity is not only a global ideal, but an important Canadian initiative. We live in perilous times where theories about a clash of civilizations abound. While the world has become a global village in terms of technology, travel and trade, the same strides are not seen in the world of faith.

It seems that the most troubled areas of the world are areas involved in religious conflict. Challenges faced by people of faith are enormous, but there is light at the end of the tunnel when we realize that *"humanity is one community"* (Qur'an), and many of our concerns are similar. As people of faith, we are all concerned about truth and justice, about poverty and violence and international human rights.

I believe the clash of civilizations can be averted if we can have communication between citizens of the earth. As theologian Hans Küng has said, there can be no survival of democracy without a coalition of believers and non-believers in mutual respect.

How do we build mutual respect? In these challenging and too often troubled times, we need new perspectives and models so that we can find humane answers to the challenges of globalization, based on a deep respect for the diversity of cultures and religions in our world community. There is a desperate need for new and practical ways of reintroducing spirituality, ethics and faith into the international debate on globalization and the local consultation on inclusivity and social reform.

I believe that Canada is the model the world needs to emulate. I'm not alone in this thought. Karen Armstrong, prolific author and theologian, was invited to the launch of Women Engaging in Bridge Building on Parliament Hill, Ottawa, where she spoke about building bridges and religious inclusivity. Armstrong said that in her travels across the globe she has seen only one country where pluralism can work successfully. That country is Canada.

I am energized to see Time magazine's recent cover story, entitled, *A NATION AT PRAYER*. I don't have to tell you which nation they are talking about but if you have any doubts, just look around you and tell me honestly, which other country in the world invites its multi-faith practitioners to a discussion about religious inclusivity in the heart of its political arena?

In this issue of Time, they write about a Vision TV/Time poll which finds that 84 percent of Canadians agree that all religions have elements of truth and three quarters believe that Canada's religious diversity is a source of strength for religious beliefs...that same diversity of religious experience in Canada may be increasing our tendency to explore faith. Furthermore, six out of 10 Canadians say they are interested in learning more about other religions and spiritual matters.

To illustrate this even better, I want share with you an email I received a few days ago. I don't know the writer but it warmed my heart, reinforcing my belief in the powers of religious diversity.

The gentleman writes:

Dear Ms. Raza:
I received information that you are participating in a conference at the Episcopal Center in North Carolina at the end of January, 2004. My wife and I had the privilege of visiting Toronto recently and we met some really fine people there. I was really impressed by all the different racial and ethnic groups living in relative harmony, and at times felt like there was real brotherhood and sisterhood there. Yes, I thought Toronto was an exceptional place. Do you feel the same way about it? I am an American, born and raised in the Christian tradition, and a spiritual life is very important to me. I respect other religions as well. I am disturbed by the pointless hatred that is so prevalent in the world. As a person who wants to believe in the brotherhood of humanity despite all the evidence I see, if you think it would be worthwhile for me to attend, I will try to overcome some obstacles and come there to participate.

My answer to the writer and to you, my friends, is: Yes, you are right. While Toronto and Ontario are leaders in diversity, Canada overall is an exceptional multi-faith and multicultural mosaic. We have something quite unique in Canada and if we don't preserve, protect and promote it - we'll lose it. In the 14 years I've lived in Toronto, I've seen the growth of multi-faith groups and their freedom of religious expression. Canada has given protection to people of faith who were persecuted, sometimes in their country of birth. Here we live with freedom to practise our faith in any way we like. Differences in belief systems don't have to lead to confrontation.

In my tradition, we believe that unity of people doesn't necessarily mean their uniformity so the unique concept of a garland of different flowers making a beautiful bouquet certainly personifies what Canada means to many of us.

Canada is being plugged as an international model of a pluralistic society. People will draw upon Canadian experience to help other societies engender pluralism in their institutions, laws and policies. Forming partnerships with Canada becomes valuable for institutions and individuals, who will serve as a strategic global source of values, knowledge, experience and practices of pluralism for diverse peoples from around the world. I have been invited to speak at three conferences in 2004, in the U.S., Dubai and Spain, to talk about what makes us tick. But we can't rest on our laurels. We still have a long way to go and need to practise what we preach.

As the respected Dalai Lama said, *"It's not enough to belong to a religion. You also have to put it into practise. Religion is like a medicine. You have to ingest it to combat the illness."*

Speaking about illness, across the lakes and to the south of us, the waters are clearly murky. According to their own diversity survey, it was found that only 54 percent of the American public thinks all religions are equally true; 47 percent of respondents were of the view that the word "fanatical" applied to the religion of Islam. Nearly one quarter (23 percent) said they favoured making it illegal for Muslim groups to meet in the U.S. for worship. While perceptions of Hindus and Buddhists were more favourable, one person in five still favoured making it illegal for these groups to meet.

I can only say, Thank God for Canada, where pluralism is no longer a luxury, but has become a necessity of life. We have a choice.

You may ask, what is religious inclusivity? As a Muslim, I could say that it means inclusion of my faith in the mainstream. The good news is that I do see inclusion of my faith. Imagine my surprise when after a decade of writing about Islam and Ramadhan, I walked past the Hudson's Bay Store on Toronto's Yonge Street and saw huge posters in the windows, saying *Happy Ramadan.*

Similarly, IKEA has introduced décor for Muslim celebrations in their new brochure; the Ontario government gives Muslims vacation with pay for religious celebrations and schools reflect many of Islam's holy days. This is a small start and I'm thrilled to see the transformation.

Across the street from my home, a strip mall boasts of a *halal* meat shop alongside a lingerie store. This is the reality of pluralism in Canada.

However, the religious inclusivity we are talking about here is not just acceptance of a few faiths; rather inclusion of all faith communities that make Canada their home because each faith brings valuable reflections and expands our understanding of the human community. If we want *our* faith to be reflected in the mainstream, then we must also lobby for other faiths.

I should add here that a significant imperative of religious inclusivity is to address our mutual concerns about social justice and social reform. Together, we can work towards our common goals of eliminating homelessness, child poverty, drugs, domestic violence and the pursuit of education reforms. These issues are important to all of us and transcend barriers of faith. United, we can have a strong voice and become a force for the government to contend with.

In our pursuit of justice, we must also recognize, accept and respect the majority tradition that this country was built upon. In our rush to build bridges, we must be cautious not to harm the foundation that's already in place. The Judeo-Christian values that Canada has upheld for decades are strong values and we can add to them - not eliminate them in order to promote our own agenda. Once we start the dialogue, we'll find we have more in common than differences.

Right now, we are heading into the Christmas and Hanukah season. These festivals must be acknowledged whether we religiously celebrate them or not. Let it be politically correct to say *Merry Christmas, Happy Hanukah, Eid Mubarak* or *Happy Diwali*, instead of lumping them all together under one generic greeting of *Happy Holidays*. We must make an effort to celebrate our differences because our long-term vision should not be one of just tolerating each other. Tolerance is not inclusive, it divides. What we want to achieve is acceptance, mutual harmony and working together towards the common good.

Critics would say this is impossible. I would offer that it's already happening on a small scale. Ten years ago, did you or I know what a multi-faith or multicultural calendar was? No. But someone who cares about religious inclusivity has taken the time to reflect major faith celebrations in one joyful calendar.

In classrooms across Canada, various faiths are being recognized and celebrated. It would not be at all amiss, as far as I'm concerned, if in the public and private sector, in education and media, that a different faith is reflected, celebrated or acknowledged every day of the year. After all, students spend time and money to take a course in religions of the world. Here, all of us have the opportunity to learn about world religions without benefit of a university course.

Next, we come to the question of how religious inclusivity will take place. Can it be imposed by governments? I don't think so. Religious inclusivity only happens when faith communities and their leaders join hands with politicians to forge an understanding that through partnerships in a pluralistic society, we can encourage socially beneficial peace, nature-friendly behaviour and affirming ecumenical decisions. To be sure, many people are already committing themselves to these goals, but a deeper change of consciousness is needed. Religious inclusivity has to be promoted from the pulpit. In places of worship, whether they are churches, temples, mosques or synagogues, the message should be one of pluralism and respect.

This will help us gain respect for each other and work on the basis of common visions, ideals, values, aims and criteria. This will also help us eliminate the seed of racism, which is ignorance. We have to understand that we have the power. We need the incentive to move beyond mere tolerance towards accepting all cultures and religions.

The Aga Khan, who is the spiritual leader of the Ismaili community, is in the process of building a centre for Pluralism in Canada. In his remarks about the importance of such an institution, he said, "Fostering pluralism could be Canada's most powerful lever in enhancing its relations with all countries - in the Muslim world, in the larger developing world, and even in the West. Promoting pluralism provides an inclusive, sensitive approach to foreign relations. It means neither promulgating a single-faith/single-culture perspective, nor risking the perception that a single faith or society is being targeted for criticism. A focus on fostering pluralism would not only enhance relations between Canada and the Muslim world, it would also increase security and prosperity in Canada and around the world. Promoting pluralism could hold for Canada in the twenty-first century what peacekeeping held in the twentieth century."

REDUCING GOD TO A POLICEMAN
June 2003

Recently, I was invited by the Innoversity Summit to participate in a panel discussion on why Muslims are misrepresented by Western media. Next to me was a man, young enough to be my son, who made an excellent hi-tech presentation and at the end, when everyone was milling around, saying, "Good work," I held out my hand to congratulate him, as well. He pulled his hand back and said solemnly, with a straight face, "I don't shake hands with women."

To say I was shocked would be an understatement. Not only did I find his attitude disrespectful, I wanted to challenge him and ask why he was there; was he was afraid of women or his own sexuality? But I held my tongue because that would mean making a mockery out of Muslims, which is exactly what we were there to discuss.

As I fumed about this incident, someone kindly pointed out that certain restrictive *mis*interpretations of Islam condemn shaking hands with the opposite sex. I reminded them that people judging actions of Muslims without looking at the intention have a small view of moral and spiritual issues. Through our misinterpreted actions, we Muslims often create our own propaganda.

A few days later, I was giving a public address on Islam and women at a human rights event. A youth remarked that maybe my message would be more meaningful and have a better impact if I covered my head! At the risk of being told (which I have!) "You have amazing eye contact for a Muslim woman," I looked him straight in the eye and said, "Were you listening to the message or looking at the highlights in my hair?"

It's this kind of monitoring, rampant in our faith, that makes me wonder about bickering over mundane petty issues that reduce the status of God to a mere policeman and move us away from the beautiful message of love, compassion, justice and truth.

I made the point of telling the young man distinctly that the injunction for modesty is for both men and women. However, since Muslim men have always interpreted Islamic *shari'a* law, they spend more time telling women how to be women, thus losing sight of the actual message. In this process, I gained some valuable insight on the controversial topic of interpretation, which continues to cause confusion amongst Muslims.

A friend sent me an article by Holly Lebowitz Rossi from the Religion News Service called *"Scholars say that the Battle for the Soul of Islam Neither Accurate nor Appropriate"*. In the article, the author quotes Sulayman Nyang, professor of African and Islamic Studies at Howard University in Washington D.C., who says we should be asking who controls the power of interpretation of the Muslim belief system or *din* in Arabic. "The battle is for what that *din* means....today," Nyang says.

Nyang is obviously referring to the emerging trend in some countries to enforce *shari'a* law, as we see happening in Pakistan today. Nyang states, "There is this contestation over who defines Islam and who can use his or her interpretation of Islam to justify the right of certain people to govern." This point resonates in my conscience as I watch the so called *shari'a* laws being used to specifically target women and suppress their human rights. In some cases, women interpret *shari'a* to their own detriment, as in the case of the Muslim woman in Florida who insists on getting her driving license without a photo and has sued the state court for wishing to implement the law. (Despite the fact that thousands of Muslim women drivers who wear *hijab* have their photos on their licenses.)

My interpretation of this case is simple. Follow the laws of the land or choose to live happily in a place like Saudi Arabia, where women aren't allowed to drive at all. That is the Saudis' interpretation of the *shari'a*, along with other misogynist and harsh injunctions over women.

Amina Wadud, professor of Islamic studies at the Commonwealth University in Virginia and author of *Qur'an and Woman*, is an excellent ambassador for women's rights in Islam. Recently, she presented a paper at an international conference on AIDS and HIV held by Prime Minister Mahatir Mohamad of Malaysia, who is one of the more progressive Islamic leaders. Twenty delegates stormed out after Wadud suggested that some Islamic teachings worsen the spread of the disease. Wadud faces the wrath of the extremist conservatives who accused her of blasphemy when she said, "Islam and Muslims exacerbate the spread of AIDS and...a traditional Islamic theological response can never cure AIDS."

She explained that Muslim women are bound by Islam to comply with their husband's desire for sex and can be punished if they do not. After being accused of demonizing Islam, Wadud told reporters that she stood by her comments. "My paper just states opinions that are different from others..."

Difference of opinion has been the hallmark of Islamic jurisprudence with five accepted Muslim legal schools of thought, but the ability to accept a difference of opinion has been erased in present time.

Shari'a is a body of rules and regulations based on the Qur'an and Sunnah. To follow the *shari'a* means living a morally responsible life. It's ironical that *shari'a*, which means "the broad path leading to water" (the idea of water being fluid and flexible), has been made inflexible and rigid. It's the road of moral, ethical and just activity that all Muslims can follow wherever they live. Many Muslims practice *shari'a* while living under the Canadian Charter of Rights and Freedoms, which is not at odds with *shari'a* as it should be understood and practised. It does not have to be forced as in Nigeria, Sudan and Pakistan, where assertion of *shari'a* is a political act, which reduces women and minorities to second-class citizens.

Al-Ghazzali (d. 505/1111), one of the most famous thinkers of his time, held that each Muslim must have enough knowledge of the *shari'a* to put it into practise in his or her own life. Nevertheless, other scholars have warned against too much time implementing *shari'a* since it can blind people to the other dimensions of the religion, which are also essential. *Shari'a* cannot exist without *ijtehad* (working out principles), *ijma* (consensus), *qiyas* (analogy), and most of all - *aql* (reason).

Essentially, the laws of Islam must never be distorted to destroy the morality of Islam. Those who misuse and enforce laws in the name of Islam destroy the moral fabric of society. The president of Pakistan, Pervez Musharraf, has just warned residents of Pakistan against adopting the Taliban version of Islam in the country which is struggling for economic recovery and progress. "We are being called terrorists, fundamentalists, extremists and intolerant," Musharraf said. "We have to decide whether we need Talibanization or progressive Islam."

ORDER A FATWA
- DELIVERED IN 30 MINUTES OR IT'S FREE!
October 2003

A *fatwa* on moi? Last week I received a *fatwa* against an annual event that I host.

According to Khaled Abou El Fadl, law professor at the University of California, a *fatwa* is "a non-binding legal opinion issued in response to a legal problem."

This *fatwa* was for an event called Milaad, which features poetry or literature written in honour of the Prophet's birth, his life and achievements. Although this celebration is not an Islamic duty, it is a spiritual tradition developed by Muslims out of love and reverence for Prophet Mohammad and his family. I've celebrated and participated in Milaads since I was a child. In those days, there were no extremists hounding us.

I knew that sooner or later, some religious crank would find me but still I was surprised when I saw the email with my name on it. I'm no stranger to hostility...I've received pepper spray, crank calls and hate mail; my husband has been taken aside and asked why he "allows" his wife so much freedom to speak out; at various times people have suggested that I write under a pseudonym or change my name entirely; and my family lives in fear of my shooting from the lip, but I've never given any of this serious thought.

I give Canada credit for this honour. It's only when I came here 14 years ago that I found freedom and confidence as a Muslim woman to study and come to understand that my faith, Islam, does not bind me but frees me to pursue knowledge and strengthen my spirituality, regardless of my gender. In Canada, I've had the opportunity to meet and converse with progressive scholars like Dr. Azizah al Hibri, Dr. Abdulaziz Sachedina and Dr. Khaled Abou el Fadl, who helped me understand my faith with reason, appreciating its various nuances and diversities.

The resulting liberation of my mind has allowed me to reflect upon and critique some of the false ideologies being promoted by my co-religionists, especially those who take direction from a deviation of Islam, which forms the state religion of Saudi Arabia, and makes a mockery of our faith. This obviously has not endeared me to many who want to cling to the illusion that they are the chosen ones, and their way is the *only* way.

Since long before September 11, I've been writing and speaking about issues that we, as Muslims are grappling with. I've spoken out about injustices against women and minorities, about gender equality, against intolerance and interfaith polemics, against extremism and violence of all kinds, including suicide bombing, and most often about inflexible interpretations of Islam that force all joy out of our traditions.

Last year, just before I celebrated my annual Milaad, I found an article in an ethnic newspaper with a message from Shaykh Abdel Azeez al-Sheikh, Grand Mufti and highest religious official in Saudi Arabia. He blasted these celebrations as heresy and condemned them as "mimicking Christians." So, I promptly wrote an article in The Toronto Star and explained the history of the Milaad tradition, placing it at the time of the Prophet and explaining that it is a custom that was developed out of love for our Prophet. I thought I had made my point and could rest easy.

But the policing does not stop. This year, my email invitation for Milaad made its way to an organization in America called the American Muslim Association of North America - the Islamic Center for Reaching and Preaching. Al-Amana boasts of a *fatwa* service. *Fatwas* by Al-Amana Shura advisors.

"We search before giving a *fatwa*," they proudly declare on their web site.

Wow. I'm impressed. Despite the countless people indulging in devious activities, they found little ole me to send their *fatwa* to. According to their long, boring, email (which is adapted from Majmoo Fatawa Samahat al-Shaykh Abdel Aziz ibn Baz), I've received ruling number 2/882.

What an enriching life these guys must lead. They even have a toll free number, 1-800-95-FATWA !

They should know that it will take more than a *fatwa* to deter me. So I had my celebration over the weekend. What better way to celebrate Thanksgiving than a thank you to God over samosas and tea, with my friends, family and well wishers, including men who came to show support.

If organizations like Al-Amana are allowed to exist freely in North America, then I would like to see *fatwas* issued against governments who allow:

- Subjugation of their entire female populous
- Killing of journalists
- Persecution of minorities
- Waging war against innocent men, women and children

DO MUSLIMS EAT KETCHUP? DIVERSITY IN ISLAM
November 2003

In the course of my interfaith outreach, I've been asked many leading questions, including, "Who is a Muslim?" and "Do Muslims eat ketchup?"

The short answer to the first question is: a Muslim is a person who shovels the snow off his neighbour's driveway and yes, we love ketchup and tomatoes, provided you're not throwing them at us.

More frequently, people ask me why I do this work. I found the answer in an article by Karen Armstrong, theologian and prolific author. She says, "Every time a violent action or an intolerant word is spoken, the world becomes a worse place and the virus of evil and hatred spreads. But every time any single believer reaches out to others in compassion and sympathy, the world improves a bit."

This is what I believe my purpose is - to reach out and communicate that we have much to share in our heritage and traditions, provided we take time to understand each other.

My multi-faith perspective began at a young age. I studied in a convent and learned the Lord's Prayer before I learned my own Muslim prayers. It doesn't seem to have damaged my psyche.

I'm here to do damage control and correct some common fallacies about Islam and Muslims. This dialogue comes at a significant time for Canadians, when Eastern religions, Buddhism, Hinduism and Islam, are the fastest growing religions in the country, with the number of Muslims having doubled in the last decade.

Islam is the faith of 1.3 billion followers worldwide, one in every five human beings. Nearly four million Muslims live in North America. The Western media make it obvious that a better understanding of Islam is warranted. Whatever you do, please don't learn your Islam from CNN.

From Samarkand to Spain and beyond, Islamic civilizations have produced great works of science, art, geography, medicine and philosophy, which, in turn, have made vital contributions to Western culture. These Muslim societies included sizeable and prosperous populations of Buddhists, Christians, Hindus, Jews and Zoroastrians - proof of the inclusive character of Islamic civilizations.

Therefore, the so-called Muslim world is not monolithic. With more than 182 million Muslims, Indonesia has the world's largest Muslim population, followed by Pakistan, India, Bangladesh and Turkey. Nonetheless, history and geopolitics (reinforced by recent crises) have often led Western observers to equate the Muslim world solely with the Arab world or the Middle East. All Arabs are not Muslim and all Muslims are not Arab. As a matter of fact, there are also Arab Christians and Arab Jews.

From Albania to Zanzibar, Muslims come from a tremendous diversity of backgrounds and speak a variety of languages, including Bengali, Chinese, Swahili, Persian, Turkish and English.

Recent global events have been framed as a clash of civilizations between the Muslim world and the Judeo-Christian West. This thesis is constructed on a faulty premise, one that sees Islam and the West as somehow having developed in isolation. To talk about such a clash is to make the fundamental mistake of forgetting the common basis of Western and Muslim civilizations.

Russell Baker, a New York Times journalist, points out that North America no longer boasts only a Judeo-Christian majority. North Americans should now be correctly referred to as people following a Judeo-Christian-Islamic tradition.

Two recent meetings in Washington, one hosted by Muslims and the other by a Jewish congregation, illustrate the heightened interest in exploring theological issues together. More than 700 people assembled in the sanctuary of Washington Hebrew Congregation, the area's largest Reform congregation, for a lecture by author Bruce Feiler on his book, *Abraham: A Journey to the Heart of Three Faiths.*

The gathering was the first of 100 interfaith Abraham Summits planned in communities across the country in connection with the book's publication. The book examines the man revered by Jews, Christians and Muslims as the father of monotheism. "At the heart of his story is unity," Feiler told the audience.

"At this time in history, it's either brotherhood or other-hood," he said. Differences in how the three faiths interpret God's message is natural, Feiler noted, drawing laughs as he commented, "As the father of four children, I don't see any contradiction in making one promise to one child and another promise to another child."

In the Qur'an, Jews and Christians are referred to as *ahl al kitaab* or people of the book. The Qur'an says, "*Muhammad is but a messenger, before whom other messengers were sent*", so Muslims are instructed to appeal to the people of book through what is common between them and Islam.

Another verse in the Qur'an says, "*Say o people of the book - come to common terms as between us and you: that we have to worship none but God, that we associate no partners with him, that we erect not from among ourselves Lords and patrons other than God.*"

So, instead of enhancing our differences, we can concentrate on strengthening our common goals.

The Qur'an tells us that our challenge is not to eliminate or hide differences but to live with them. Unity of human beings does not mean their uniformity. The Qur'an says, "*O people we have formed you into nations and tribes so that you may know one another - not to conquer, convert, subjugate, revile or slaughter but to reach out with intelligence and understanding.*"

In Islam, we address God as *Allah* in our prayers, which is an Arabic word directly translating into God with no gender specification. But we are also asked to reach out to God through 99 divine attributes or names.

Most of these attributes reflect God's love, compassion and mercy for His people. The best way to experience the love of God is to love His creatures.

The understanding is that if we wish for God to be compassionate and merciful towards us, we must show the same compassion, mercy and respect towards His creation, which is all of humanity, the environment and animals. This compassion can't be selective for just a chosen few; it has to be for all.

The more we reach out to other human beings, the more we become a receiver and transmitter of God's radiance. In this way, we are drawn towards the source of all light - God, the almighty.

As an example of social justice and ethical values, Islam, like other Abrahamic religions before it, teaches us that God is just and the implementation of justice is part of God's purpose for human societies. As Muslims, we are charged with the duty of leading moral and upright lives. We are instructed not only to love one another, but to share the pain of our fellow citizens on earth.

Islam is a continuation of the Abrahamic tradition traced through Abraham's son, Ismail (Ishmael). It is the youngest of the three monotheistic faiths. Muslims believe the reason that Mohammad asked

Muslims to pray towards Mecca, when they used to pray towards the Dome of the Rock in Jerusalem, was to draw people back to the spirit of Abraham, who lived before the arrival of the Torah and the Gospel and built the *Kaaba* as the first sanctuary to one God, not for any established religion.

The Qur'an reminds us to respect people of other faiths. God states clearly in the Qur'an: *"Have faith in God and in that which has been sent down on Abraham, Ishmael, Isaac and Jacob and the tribes and that which was given to Moses and Jesus and the Prophets by their Lord. We make no distinction among any of them and to Him we have submitted."*

Pope John Paul II said, while speaking to young Muslims in Morocco, "Christians and Muslims have many things in common as believers and as human beings. We live in the same world, marked by many signs of hope, but also by multiple signs of anguish. For us, Abraham is a model of faith in God, of submission to His will and of confidence in his goodness. We believe in the same God, the one God, the living God, the God who created the world and brings His creatures to perfection."

It often surprises Christians that Jesus is mentioned more times by name in the Qur'an than the Prophet Mohammad. The Qur'an contains an entire chapter named *Mary*, regarding the birth of Jesus.

The Qur'an says, *"lakum dinakum walayadin" (to you, your faith and to me, mine)*. It is a recorded tradition that a man came to the messenger of God, Mohammad, and said, "I have accepted Islam but my sons still follow the Christian faith. Please empower them to convert. Mohammad told him not to force his sons to change their faith. He recited, *"La Ikra fi deen (there is no compulsion in religion)*, which was a message sent to Mohammed by God through the angel Gabriel, with the understanding that God knows what is in people's hearts and is the implementer of justice and mercy.

Sadly, some people breach the right to define the parameters of divine justice, and inflict satanic destruction on human society in the name of the faith.

Religion, like any other human activity, can and has been abused to denigrate and even persecute others.

The Qur'an says, *"and slay not the life which Allah has made sacred, save in the course of justice."* This means that killing one person is like killing all of humanity.

SPIRITUAL JIHAD

In the same essence, suicide is not permissible in Islam under any circumstance because Muslims believe God gives life and takes life.

Truth and justice are two key themes in the Qur'an. In chapter 10, we read that *"God never considers it permissible to act unjustly towards his creation - it is rather people who render oppression and injustice."*

Islam teaches us to differentiate between right and wrong, between good and evil. There is a verse in the Qur'an that translates: *"enjoin the good and condemn that which is evil"* - cautioning us at the same time to condemn the act and not the person committing it.

There are no grey areas in our understanding of the difference between justice and injustice, combatant and non-combatant, legitimate and illegitimate use of force. As Muslims, we have been given very clear parameters.

The Qur'an says, *"The Islamic relationship between individuals and nations is one of peace."* Muslims learn from the Qur'an that God's objective in creating the human race in different communities was so that they could relate to each other peacefully.

Having said this, it is important to mention that the Qur'an also talks about war as a contingency. When the Qur'an was revealed, warfare was a way of life and desperate business in the Arabian Peninsula. A chieftain was not expected to spare survivors after a battle. In the Qur'an, the only permissible war is one of self-defence. Muslims may not begin hostilities. *"War is always considered evil, but sometimes a war becomes the only solution to persecution and oppression."*

There were strict guidelines to war. The Prophet told his companions that they could not harm civilians, old people, children or people engaged in worship, nor could they destroy crops or animals. Life and property of all, Muslim and non-Muslim, are sacred. The Prophet said: *"truly your blood, your property and your honour are inviolable."*

The Qur'an says, *"God commands men to act with justice and virtue and enjoins upon them generosity to kinsfolk. He forbids them evil deeds and oppression He admonishes you out of His mercy, so that you may accept His advice."*

The understanding is that Islam rejects certain individuals or nations being favoured because of their wealth, power or race. God created human beings as equal who are to be distinguished from each other, only based on their faith and piety. The Prophet Mohammad said: *"O People your God is one and your forefather Adam is one. An Arab is not better than a non-Arab,* and a non-Arab is not better than an Arab; and a white person is not better than a black person and a black person is not better than a white person - except in piety."

Islam teaches us that we should be just, even with those whom we hate, as God says "and let not the hatred of others make you avoid justice. Be just: that is nearer to piety."

The burning question is: What has so galvanized the violent tendencies in Islam that the faith has been transformed from a religion of love to a culture of hate?

The answer is very complex. It is rooted in social, political and theological issues.

Stephen Schwartz, in his book, *Intellectuals and Assassins*, writes: "Throughout History, political extremists of all faiths have willingly given up their lives simply in the belief that by doing so, whether in bombings or in other forms of terror, they would change the course of history, or at least win an advantage for their cause."

Karen Armstrong writes in her book, *The Battle for God*, "Every fundamentalist movement I have studied in Judaism, Christianity and Islam is convinced that liberal, secular society is determined to wipe out religion." She continues to analyze that fighting, as they imagine, a battle for survival, fundamentalists often feel justified in ignoring the more compassionate principles of their faith.

The theologically based attitudes of these absolute puritans are at odds, not only with a Western way of life, but also with the very idea of an international society or the notion of universal human values.

In amplifying the more aggressive passages that exist in all of our scriptures, the religious extremists distort the tradition and implement hardships and restrictions on women, which are not in any way or form part of the faith.

At the time of the revelation, Islam came as a saviour for women who were sold as slaves or buried alive in Arabia. Islamic injunctions gave women freedom, equality, the right to vote, own property, do business and not be obligated to hand over their earnings. They were also given freedom of choice in marriage and divorce. Unfortunately, there has remained a huge gap in the preaching and practise of Islam in the sphere of women's issues.

In Islam, there is no formalized priesthood, so the Qur'an is open to individual interpretation. There are religious scholars, called *ulema*, who are experts in the scripture, so Muslims are advised to choose an Imam or leader from amongst them, based on their piety and expertise in both secular and scriptural subjects.

Arabic is a rich and diverse language in which one word can have ten meanings or interpretations and needs to be understood in proper historical context and supported by practise and tradition of the Prophet, called *Sunnah*.

The ability of human beings to interpret texts is both a blessing and a burden. It is a blessing because it provides us with the flexibility to adapt texts to changing circumstances. It is a burden because the reader must take responsibility for the normative values he or she brings to the text. Any text provides possibilities for meaning, not inevitabilities. Those possibilities can be exploited or developed by the reader's good faith. In other words, the meaning of the text is only as moral as the reader.

Misguidance is a universal phenomenon found in the outside world and within ourselves. Linking terrorism to Islam is like linking Pearl Harbour to Buddhism, Timothy McVeigh to Christianity or calling Baruch Goldstein, who shot 29 worshippers in the Hebron mosque, a true martyr of Israel.

Similarly, guidance is also a universal phenomenon. In other words, the human race is not conceivable without both prophets and satans.

This leaves most of us between a rock and hard place. While we condemn acts of terrorism and sympathize with the victims, we find war against innocent civilians is not the solution to any problem.

War is a state of mind well-echoed in the UNESCO constitution, which notes, "Since wars begin in the minds of men, it is in the minds of men that the defence of peace must be constructed."

In his message for the World Day of Peace on January 1, 2002, Pope John Paul II said, "No peace without justice, no justice without forgiveness."

This is the message of the ancient prophets and the bedrock of every true religion and true morality. The Prophet of Islam always looked for ways to eradicate injustice and inequity, looking upon them as the root cause of most evils.

The Pope went on to say that all world religions must cooperate to eliminate the social and cultural causes of terrorism by teaching the greatness and dignity of the human person and by spreading a clearer sense of the openness of the human family.

As an ancient poet once expressed it:

If there is light in the soul, there will be beauty in the person
If there is beauty in the person, there will be harmony in the house
If there is harmony in the house, there will be order in the nation
If there is order in the nation, there will be peace in the world.

AMERICAN MUSLIM CONVERT CRITIQUES MOSQUE CULTURE
April 2004

It has been two decades since academic and author Jeffrey Lang made the passage from atheist to devout Muslim, yet he remains as passionate as ever about his conversion.

Born to a Roman Catholic family in Bridgeport, Connecticut in 1954, Lang spent his early years questioning the existence of God and finding no satisfactory answers.

"I rebelled against all the institutions that society held sacred, including the Catholic Church," Lang said in a recent talk to Toronto's Forum for Learning, where he spoke from the heart about his passage from questioning to conviction and from bitterness to belief.

His abusive home life with an alcoholic father led to more bitterness, so at 16, Lang publicly declared himself an atheist.

In 1982, at age 28, Lang accepted Islam, based primarily on a chance reading of the Qur'an.

As Lang became a practicing Muslim, he also experienced the challenges of being a convert, both from within and outside the community.

"It's lonely being a convert to Islam," he said in an interview following his address. "I felt vulnerable and disconnected from the host community and needed support.

"The Muslim community was somewhat critical that I wasn't conservative enough and that there was no physical change in my appearance...but I didn't become Muslim to enter into a community - I already had a family. I wanted to be accepted as I am and this was a challenge."

To address these challenges, Lang wrote *Struggling to Surrender - Some Impressions of an American Convert to Islam*, in which he also tackled the rigidity of the mosque culture.

"At first, I used to attend mosque for the five daily prayers and I loved going there, but once I got married and had girls, they were not welcome at the mosque," he wrote.

"I would like to see mosques being more family friendly. Presently they are like a men's club."

Lang has three daughters ages 17, 16 and 14. "Without me, my girls would lose their only link with Islam and I don't want that to happen."

After his book was published, Lang received hundreds of e-mails, letters and phone calls.

"Mostly from atheists, converts and second-generation Muslims (living in the West) who also feel alienated from the mosque culture," he said.

His latest book, *Losing My Religion: A Call for Help* is based on the feedback he received from second-generation Muslims.

It illustrates that Lang has grown increasingly concerned about the future of young Muslims in America. He says many do not feel welcome at the mosques and are falling away from the faith.

He suggests the mosque should be a place for spiritual education and bonding. "Cultural traditions that are nonessential need to be removed. Mosques should not become a cultural asylum."

In the recently published book, Lang has offered solutions.

"Take back the mosque," he says. "Don't give it up or smother Islam - that will keep our children away. Make it user-friendly, let women become an essential part of the mosque."

His wife is on the board of directors for their local mosque.

After his talk in Toronto, as Lang was autographing books for his audience, a young man came up to him and said, "Dr. Lang you've made a believer of me. I was an atheist but now I want to revisit my faith."

Lang had a very positive experience in Canada and upon his return to Kansas, wrote to say, "Many Muslims from around the world have expressed to me their hopes that the U.S.A. Muslim community will lead the way toward Islamic reform, but I keep responding that my hopes are in Canada.

"This latest trip has left me all the more convinced that Canada is where to look for an Islamic reformation.

"I only hope our community in the U.S. gets dragged along."

THE WISDOM OF LISTENING, THE POWER OF COMMITTMENT THE WORLD PARLIAMENT OF RELIGIONS - PATHWAYS TO PEACE
July 2004

"There will be no peace among nations without peace among the religious" - Hans Küng

I had just finished performing my Friday prayers on the shores of the Mediterranean Sea. As I looked around me, I was filled with the wonder of being here, a long way from my native Pakistan and my adopted home, Canada.

I was in Barcelona to attend the Fourth Parliament of World Religions with two Canadian friends and partners in interfaith, Rev. Dr. Karen Hamilton, a practicing Christian, and Barbara Siddiqui, born in Midland, Ontario as a Christian and now a practicing Muslim.

It was an unusual situation in many ways. Two Caucasian women wearing *shalwar qameez* (Pakistani garb) were praying with me, along with a host of diverse Muslims in a VIP tent set up by the Sikh community of Birmingham, England. We were joined by local media keen to see how Muslims pray. (Thank God men and women prayed together that day!) The media were thoroughly confused when a turbaned Sikh and some non-Muslims came and joined the prayer.

This was interfaith at its best. The ad-hoc Imam said in his sermon, "Humanity is one community," and certainly at this point in time, anyone would agree.

The 2004 Parliament of World Religions was organized in partnership with the Universal Forum of Cultures – Barcelona 2004, which runs from May to September and in association with the UNESCO Centre of Catalonia. Eight thousand religious and spiritual practitioners from all over the world converged to greet and meet each other in peace. Four-hundred carefully selected seminars, workshops, performances and films were offered in the PWR program. They addressed three core themes: sustainable development, cultural diversity and conditions for peace through spiritual practice, religious identity and intra- and inter-religious dialogue. The Forum was supported by the presence of people like The Archbishop of Barcelona, Dr. Abdullah Omar Nasseef (President of the Muslim World Congress), Ela Gandhi (granddaughter of Mahatama Gandhi), Rabbi Henry J. Sobel (Chief Rabbi of Brazil) and many more.

What was I doing there? I've been dabbling in interfaith dialogue since I moved to Canada in 1989, but September 11 threw me into the heart of interfaith dialogue. In 2003, I saw a call for papers for PWR. I immediately contacted my partners in interfaith dialogue, Karen and Barbara, and said, "I'm going. Are you coming with me?" They were thrilled at the opportunity.

Of course, the fact that the venue was Barcelona only added to our desire to be there. We worked together on a proposal titled *Keeping the Path Clear - Women Engaging in Inter-faith, Inter-action and Inter-relationships*. By June, 2004, we hadn't heard back from PWR but we decided to go anyway. At the end of June, I was looking through the online program and I found our names. Our proposal had been accepted!

For me, this was a journey from the heart. Whenever I read or talked about Muslim history, I used to imagine the rich Muslim, Jewish and Christian heritage of Spain, when the three faiths lived in harmony and reached out to each other spiritually and intellectually. Here was a chance to promote that same essence of pluralism and I felt especially blessed to be chosen for this opportunity. It was only later I discovered how fortunate we were to be selected from among the thousands of proposals that were submitted.

On our first day in Barcelona, Barb, Karen and I took the metro to the Forum site. On the metro we met a South Asian couple wearing PWR badges and we chatted. As we exchanged names, the lady said, "So you are Raheel Raza?" I was a bit shocked. She was the vice president of PWR and she knew me through our proposal, which she said she personally approved because there weren't too many Muslim women presenters from North America. We were thrilled and humbled at the same time, to be invited to present along with theologians like Hans Küng and Tariq Ramadan, Nobel Peace Prize laureate Adolfor Perez Esquivel (the Portuguese writer), activists like Susan George and authors like Deepak Chopra. This was a gift.

The Forum site was a 30-hectare space next to the Mediterranean Sea and an extension of the waterfront that began with the 1992 Olympic Games. It was a sight for sore eyes and hearts. There was a sea of people in the colours of the world; dresses, voices, faces of diversity. The orange robes of Buddhist monks mingled with the white dresses of the Sufis. Everyone stopped and wished each other in peace, smiled and sometimes spontaneously hugged each other. This was beyond tolerance; it was embracing each other.

Throughout the Forum site there were four major exhibitions, 22 smaller shows, 400 concerts, 170 music groups, 60 street performances and four circuses. Everywhere were interactive installations, markets, games and fun. High-tech, well organized events manned by hundreds of youth volunteers from all over the world were exceptional.

Our trio caused some surprise. A yogi nun from America told me she had never met such strong Muslim women before and she hoped we would change the world!

Shirin Ebadi, 2003 Nobel Peace Prize laureate, stated in the opening of the Parliament of the World's Religions, "Human rights cannot be protected with bombs" and denounced the despotic behaviour of those "who ignore human rights and democracy with the argument of belonging to a different culture and shadow dictatorial regimes with religious and nationalistic arguments."

In her address speech, Ebadi defended Islam, declaring it is compatible with respect for human rights and democracy. She showed her disagreement with the Islamic declaration of human rights. In her opinion, "if each of the 5,000 religions of the world made their own declaration, this would be the end of the Universal Declaration of Human Rights."

She went on to say, "God has made human beings different but the ultimate goal of all religions is the pursuit of happiness and thus all religions can share the things they have in common."

We attended as many dialogue sessions as we could, sometimes together and other times separately. But we always met for lunch at the same place, The Parliament by the Sea. This was a tent city set up on the seashore of the sea by the Sikh community of Birmingham, U.K. Here, volunteers from the Sikh community, ages 16 to 60, first welcomed people, then poured water on their hands, gave people headscarves and served lunch, drinks and water. They catered to nearly 6,000 people each day. They also invited participants to pray in their scared spaces tent. My longing for *desi* food was quenched with *pooris* (fried bread), *daal* (lentils), *chawal* (rice) and *achaar* (pickle).

Our presentation was slotted for Saturday, July 10 at 11:30 a.m. We arrived there early, nervous because we had no way of knowing how many people would attend. To our delight, a trustee from PWR came to introduce our session and told us how important it was to acknowledge the work we are doing. We felt honoured. Our room soon filled with diverse people, including some Barcelona Muslims. Karen, Barb and I spoke about the interfaith work we do and why we do it. At the end of our session, we distributed little boxes containing a Canadian maple syrup candy, a Canada pin and a message saying "Pray for Peace – Act for Peace", while we played Dawud Wharnsaby's song called *People of the Boxes* from the CD, *The Prophet's Hands*.

Later, people came up to ask us questions. A man wearing an Arab dress and a *kufi*, came to me, blessed me for the work we do and to my surprise, had tears running down his face as he said, "You make me proud to be Muslim." It wasn't the only time in Barcelona that I felt touched to tears.

The same evening, the City of Barcelona had arranged for A Communities Night so that people of faith could meet their own communities in different parts of the city. Barbara and I went to Ramlas Raval and met the Barcelona Muslim community. There is a large Arab and Pakistani community active in Barcelona and the Imams of two mosques gave talks condemning violence and terrorism, which was heartening to hear. We learned that after the Madrid train bombing, people of all faiths had joined together in Barcelona, engaging in candlelight vigils for peace.

On the following night, there was a Sacred Music concert at the Sagrada Familia (The Sacred Family) Cathedral, which is one of the most outstanding landmarks of Barcelona. It was built by renowned architect Antoni Gaudi and is still unfinished. In this awe-inspiring structure, 10 religious traditions presented music, movement, meditation and chants. It was an unforgettable experience, sitting under the clear skies while the cathedral resonated with the sounds of the Cor Gospel of Barcelona; Ang singing from India; Sheva, a Jewish-Muslim band with roots in Hebrew, Arabic and Tribal cultures and Ushaq, the rich musical legacy of the Sufi Mevlevi order. As the Sufis started chanting *Allah Hu*, there was a hush, and then a few people joined in and I trembled as I heard more than half the audience chanting with the Sufis. The concert ended with 10 children of 10 traditions holding up peace lights.

After a week of debates centered on commitments on the issues of religious violence, access to safe water, the fate of refugees worldwide and the elimination of developing countries' debts, the PWR came to a close. Religious leaders who convened the gathering deemed the event a success.

Dirk Ficca, executive director of the Council for PWR, said that one fundamental difference between this gathering and others discussing the same subjects was that "when people of faith commit to address religious violence and other pressing issues facing the global community, they follow through. We make a commitment not only to the world, but out of a deeply rooted religious or spiritual conviction. That is what makes the Barcelona Parliament commitments so special, and why this year's Parliament in Barcelona is going to make an impact."

BEYOND THE FLUFF STUFF
September 2004

We live in times that boggle our minds and try our souls. Times when a culture of hatred has taken precedence over our traditions of peace, love and tolerance. Usually, a sentence that begins with the words "an Imam, a Rabbi and a Priest..." is the opening line of a joke. These days, the grouping of religions is a serious matter.

It is empowering to see that institutions like churches and mosques are taking the initiative to know each other. We need more open doors.

Interfaith needs to be done at an individual level, in every aspect of our lives. Faith leaders should lead the way and talk more about the interfaith objective at every opportunity. For Muslims, knowing their spiritual neighbours is an inherent part of the faith.

A specific process needs to be put into place through workshops or seminars, where Muslims can be given guidelines on how to participate in interfaith.

Why is guidance necessary when interfaith relations are built into the Muslim faith? Through my own experience, I've learned this: Interfaith is not everyone's cup of tea.

There is an old Arabic proverb: words from lips reach the ears, but words from the heart reach the heart. Interfaith has to come from the heart.

Some people think that interfaith is a competition and take an aggressive stance: My god is better than your god. They believe interfaith is not for them.

As Karen Armstrong, who calls herself a freelance monotheist, says so beautifully, "We need humility before knowledge – we have to kill our ego and only then can sincere and true interfaith take place."

Knowledge, also known as a weapon of mass instruction, is essential to interfaith dialogue. This knowledge is not only of those we think of as "the other" but also of ourselves. Intra-faith dialogue needs to happen alongside inter-faith dialogue. If we don't know ourselves, how can we extend ourselves to others outside our tradition?

In guiding our community towards interfaith, the first step is to create trust. Trust comes when we look for commonalities and similarities. I have met people who think interfaith means highlighting the differences in faith traditions. While there is no compromising of principles, I believe that all faith traditions have a lot more in common than they have differences. It's just easier to point out the differences. But when we take the time and effort to talk about similarities, it builds trust, educates and informs.

Once we establish trust, we need to move to a higher level of dialogue which I call Beyond the Fluff Stuff. It is not just discussion about religious holidays, but ongoing dialogue about some of the more difficult issues which we don't wish to sweep under the table but need to debate in a civilized manner in an atmosphere of respect and trust.

For example, my group of interfaith women did a panel of the parts of our scriptures that we have difficulty in interpreting. We discovered that in the three monotheistic traditions, our concerns were similar, so we began to relate at a different level of understanding.

I have a bumper sticker on my car that says "Those who pray together stay together." This is an important discovery on the journey to interfaith. How often do we pray together?

In Barcelona, Spain, at the Parliament of World Religions in 2004, we did pray together. Praying together removes insecurity and fear and helps people understand that interfaith does not mean conversion.

Further to knowledge, I have a recommendation for Canada's educational system. I believe some study of religion needs to be made part of the curriculum in junior schools. I know there are a few groups working towards this and I support their initiative because even in secular terms, this is about the history of the world. I know comparative religion is taught in high school but I think that is rather late. In the Canadian mosaic, children are exposed to diverse faiths every day of their lives (except those in very isolated and elite private educational systems), so an understanding of other faiths can only create tolerance and respect.

Faith is a four letter word in the media, so interfaith doesn't make good news because it is warm and fuzzy and brings people together, which doesn't sell newspapers. Note how much coverage a racial or religiously motivated crime will get as compared to an event such as the Parliament of World Religions in Barcelona. It was the largest interfaith gathering in the world and barely made international news. We have to empower media to support the interfaith work happening at many levels and write to our local media about such events.

We must also understand that interfaith is not a one-time solution. Neither is it a band-aid solution. It needs to be worked at consistently, persistently and continuously to make a difference in a world that has been torn by religious strife.

MERRY CHRISTMAS FROM A MERRY MUSLIM
December 2004

With the rapid spread of foot-in-mouth disease by the religious right and the righteously religious from Washington to Waterloo via Vancouver, I can't think of a better time to come out of the closet as a Merry Muslim.

To acknowledge that I love this time of year and have already been an active participant in the launch of the Christmas season is challenging to say the least. I say *Merry Christmas* with feeling since I recently celebrated my own festival of Eid on November 15, wished my Hindu and Sikh friends a delightful Diwali on November 12 and was invited to a Hanukkah celebration this week. So I feel I can participate in celebrations for Christmas with my Christian colleagues and friends who, we should remember, form the majority in Canada.

Before people get their knickers in a knot and slap *fatwa* #2 on my head (I received *fatwa* #1 last year for celebrating the birth of my own Prophet), let me clarify that I indulge in celebrations of the cultural and non-alcoholic kind, keeping my feet firmly grounded in my own faith. In fact, it is because of my religious convictions that I feel it is important to greet others on their day of celebration.

Last month, the Ontario provincial plaque marking the hundredth anniversary of the Santa Claus Parade was unveiled, and I was front and centre as a volunteer. Wrapped in my deepest red shawl, red jingly reindeer antlers perched on my head, I spent the afternoon in Toronto's Nathan Philips Square shaking my bells to Christmas carols sung by the St. Michael's Choir School.

I was honoured to be part of this event, which highlighted the history of the parade. It was delightful to see and feel the enthusiasm of the choir, a multicultural group of young, talented kids who were my responsibility to organize. When the surprise guest, Santa, emerged from Toronto City Hall, I cheerfully posed for photos.

This is when I was fondly dubbed the Merry Muslim, which I take as a compliment since I have long tried to get everyone to say *Merry Christmas* instead of *Happy Holidays*.

A Muslim friend who is an elementary school principal decorates her office and talks during assembly about each specific holiday as it is observed. This, she says, is like anti-racism instruction and a lesson in world religions. From aboriginal students to Zoroastrians, everyone's culture and faith is celebrated, including, of course, Christmas. She admits it is a lot of work, but it keeps her school in a constant state of celebration.

How inspiring. I wish we did this in our workplaces where people get hot under the collar over calling things by their proper names. I am on the committee organizing our Christmas celebration at work - and I refuse to call it anything other than *Christmas*.

Ironically, my colleagues on the committee are all Christians who are trying to convince me that calling our event a Christmas party won't be acceptable to all. I remind them that people around the globe, from Afghanis to Zambians, call December 25 *Christmas*, whether they celebrate it or not.

So please, let's call Christmas by its real name. By sharing one another's faith and culture, we can promote goodwill and good cheer.

SHARI'A: IT'S ABOUT RELIGIOUS FREEDOM
December 2004

Yesterday, former attorney-general Marion Boyd released her report, *Dispute Resolution in Family Law: Protecting Choice, Promoting Inclusion*. In her report to the Ontario government, Boyd recommended, "The Arbitration Act should continue to allow disputes to be arbitrated using religious law." Boyd advised that Ontario Muslims be given the same rights as Roman Catholics and Jews when seeking arbitration based on religious law for family disputes and inheritance cases.

Before I had a chance to read it, I received a voice mail from a television reporter, saying, "I'd like your comments *against shari'a* law and how it discriminates against Muslims women's rights."

I called back and said, "It's rather presumptuous of you to assume that I'm against *shari'a*. If you call me back, I can tell you the positive aspects of *shari'a*."

I wasn't surprised that the reporter didn't phone back.

Within 24 hours of the report being released, I've heard a slew of uninformed and biased ideas ranging from calling anyone in favour of religious arbitration a fundamentalist to labelling Marion Boyd a white racist. The groups opposing the establishment of a Muslim Tribunal have effectively fanned the flames of Islamophobia and taken us back to the dark times immediately following 9/11.

Since the hot debate on establishment of a Muslim Arbitration Tribunal started almost a year ago, I've been concerned about where this is taking us. Everywhere I've been invited to speak on Islam, concern has been expressed about Canada supporting a Taliban-like regime. The reality is that Ismaili Muslims have been successfully using arbitration and mediation for some time, just like our counterparts in the Jewish and Catholic community.

The public doesn't focus on the fact that this is not about *shari'a* but about religious freedom. Unfortunately, the word *shari'a* has been bandied about and grossly misused. Dr. Lynda Clarke, professor of Religion at Concordia University, explains, "Islamic law as an ideal pattern of life desired by God is known as *shari'a*, i.e. "the way". All Muslims aspire toward *shari'a*; but it can never fully be known by the limited human intellect. Islamic law as understood and applied is therefore called *fiqh*. *Fiqh* means, literally, "understanding". This understanding is acknowledged to be human, fallible, diverse, and to an extent (the extent is disputed) flexible and changeable. Consequently, there is a very wide range of understanding of law in the Muslim tradition, and different applications of law in the Muslim world."

To me, *shari'a* is also the core value system for Muslims; it's a code of moral and ethical values that we implement into our daily lives in many different ways. In terms of birth, death and marriage, even secular Muslims often fall back on *shari'a*.

Regarding women's rights, an in-depth study of Islamic law will show that it gave Muslim women rights, based on knowledge of the society they lived in. Fourteen-hundred years ago, *shari'a* gave women rights to inheritance, voting, decisions in marriage and divorce. Judith Tucker's book, *In the House of the Law*, highlights how *shari'a* courts were favourable to women during the Ottoman rule.

I understand and appreciate the fears of women who have personally been subjected to male patriarchal injustice in countries that use *shari'a* as a crutch to legitimize their oppression of women. This is why it is imperative to separate culture and politics from the faith and take a balanced approach without resorting to hysterics and polemics.

As a person keenly involved in the development of Canadian Muslims and being on record as having spoken out against gender apartheid, I'm not blindly supporting the Muslim Tribunal. As Dr. Clarke argues, "for any group to claim that *their* fiqh (understanding) amounts fully and unmistakably to *shari'a* is, in my view, contrary to the workings and spirit of the Islamic legal tradition."

Therefore, I believe it is important for the Tribunal to reflect the diversity and flexibility of Islamic law. To achieve this, much work has to be done to create awareness and educate the Muslim community.

One relevant issue raised by the opponents of the Tribunal is that uneducated immigrant Muslim women may not know their rights under Islam and might be coerced into decisions that go against them. However, these women probably don't know what their rights are under Canadian law - a challenge faced by most immigrant communities.

Herein lies a unique opportunity to educate, inform and bring about that change. We can enlist help from enlightened Muslims as well as the Canadian government so that values and respect of both systems are set in place. This will help oversee that we don't fall into the same pattern as Saudi Arabia, Pakistan or Iran.

Shari'a and Islam must not be presented as murky and open to the prejudice that lurks on the surface. There is room in Canada for religious arbitration and secular law without encroaching on each other. Most of all, let us remember religious arbitration is a personal choice.

EID AND AWE IN NEW YORK
March 2005

Eid. A word that means joy. It's the feast after the fast, a major celebration for Muslims after fasting in the month of Ramadan. Deciding to spend Eid in New York this past weekend turned out to be a joyous decision on my part, and while tradition has it that Eid lasts for three days, I celebrated in a variety of ways for the whole week.

But I'm getting ahead of myself.

I went to NYC ostensibly to attend the launch of the Progressive Muslims Union of North America. I arrived two days early. My hosts in Manhattan are part of a group that had decided that through science and technology, Ramadan and Eid can be predicted in advance of physical moon sighting, so that Muslims can begin and end together. The decision was for a Sunday Eid and they invited me to join them at the Eid prayer and celebration.

We drove to the Dorral Arrowood Convention Center in Rye Brook, New York, where the auspicious event was arranged by the American Sufi Muslim Association (ASMA). Three-hundred men, women and children prayed together in the great ballroom, side by side, with no partition. These people have broken away from the traditional mosque culture (where usually women are relegated to another area) because they want to offer prayers with their families, friends and loved ones. They took another bold step by inviting an Imam of their choice. And what a brilliant choice!

Imam Feisal Abdul Rauf is a dynamic man with a vision as large as his heart. Author of a new book titled, *What's Right with Islam: A New Vision for Muslims in the West*, he was educated in England and Malaysia and has a degree in physics from Columbia University. Founder and CEO of ASMA and Imam of Masjid Al-Farah, a mosque in New York City, twelve blocks from Ground Zero, Imam Feisal has dedicated his life to building bridges between Muslims and the West. He is a leader in the effort to build religious pluralism and integrate Islam into modern American society.

Regarded as one of the world's most eloquent and erudite Muslim leaders, Imam Feisal is a charismatic public speaker and has appeared in national and international media, including CNN, CBS, NBC, ABC, PBS and BBC. He has been quoted in The New York Times, New York Daily News, Jerusalem Post and Associated Press.

The Imam's sermon could have been easily accepted in a church, synagogue or temple as he spoke about two kinds of religion – good and bad. He talked about Islam with a small "i" and said it means submission to God by anyone: Muslim, Christian, Jew, Buddhist. This must have sat well with John Bennet, a lone Buddhist in the congregation who heads the Cordoba Initiative. Imam Feisal is the architect of the Cordoba Initiative, an inter-religious blueprint for improving relations between America and the Muslim world and pursuing Middle East peace. As a tireless advocate for an ecumenical solution to the Israeli-Palestinian conflict, he has impressed his vision on U.S. lawmakers and administration officials, most recently as member of the National Inter-religious Initiative for Peace in Washington, D.C.

Young people surrounded the Imam after the sermon, which was unusual in itself, but the surprise did not end there for me. Following the prayer, there was brunch and *live* music. Some enthusiastic families also indulged in a bit of *bhangra* (Punjabi disco). I was also astounded to see that the Imam's wife, Daisy Khan, does not cover her head. She leads women in prayer at their mosque and is involved in interfaith dialogue at an international level. Upon my questioning, she said, "I've done my own *ijtihad* (research and reasoning) and found that modest dress is what is required so I believe this is fine for me."

I had definitely encountered progressive Muslims.

The next morning, Monday, November 15, was the official launch of The Progressive Muslims Union of North America. The Union Theological Seminary of Columbia University hosted this event in the Bonhoeffer Room (at one time called The Prophet's Chamber).

PMU is the result of months of work and planning by a diverse group of American Muslims, including renowned academics such as Omid Safi, professor of Islamic Studies at Colgate University, professionals like Hussein Ibish, communications director of the American-Arab Anti-Discrimination Committee and Sarah Eltantawi, a consultant to American organizations and communication director for PMU. There were also community activists like Ahmed Nassef, editor-in-chief of Muslim Wakeup, the world's most popular Muslim online magazine.

Sarah Eltantawi opened the media event by saying, "PMU seeks to expand the range of spiritual, social, intellectual and political choices for

North American Muslims, and to challenge the narrow set of "normative" Muslim ideas and behaviour expected of all of us both within and beyond the North American Muslim community." When asked if they are a breakaway group, she responded that the aim is not to create some sort of "new Islam" or "American Islam". "Rather, we seek to join the work already underway by so many others to bolster the sense of pluralism, commitment to justice, and diversity within Islamic discourses which has been undermined by the spread of literalist and dogmatic interpretations of the faith in recent decades."

Ahmed Nassef spoke about the four different areas that PMU will work in: arts, reform and education; spiritual awareness; and politics. He said that PMU is like a "big tent" under which they hope other existing organizations will gather to defend civil rights at home, human rights abroad and celebrate an enlightened vision of Islam.

Joining the PMU board is Torontonian Tarek Fatah, founder of the Muslim Canadian Congress, who pointed out that Canada has made great contributions to the progressive religions agenda. He started off by stating, "Canada has more to offer the U.S. than just cheap drugs for seniors. Canadians don't just pay lip service but actually practice a separation of religion and state". MCC will pursue the Canadian component of the progressive Muslim agenda here at home, not without controversy. Tarek had hardly arrived home when he was slapped with the label of being a "progressive extremist" (whatever that means).

During my interaction with other American Muslims over Eid celebrations, I heard some criticism of PMU. One was that they might compromise basic Islamic principles and "pander to western popular ideology". Others referred to this group as "being too liberal" because they feel the PMU mandate is too wide. The PMU board seemed well aware of the challenges ahead of them and said they expect the community will go through denial, anger and then hopefully acceptance when they see there is a need for reform from within.

A New York Times columnist who had come to cover the event commented that the kind of message being given by PMU through their mission statement is a discourse that is not heard in the mainstream and felt it is important to get the message out.

I found the PMU board very sincere in their efforts to try and find a balance. I fully support their mandate for exorcizing the excesses of many within the community who veer towards polemics and hate propaganda, which has no place in our faith. I applaud their decision to avoid extremism of every kind and to be inclusive, respecting the diversity of our faith, culture and traditions. My only concern is that in labelling themselves "progressive" or "moderate", is the message being given to the outside world that those who aren't part of any such organization are not progressive or moderate?

The New York Times columnist made note that none of the women who attended the PMU launch were wearing *hijab*. This bothers me because the message seems to connect head covering with being regressive and that is certainly not the case.

Another news item in mainstream media talked about young Muslims becoming extremist by "going regularly to the mosque, growing a beard and wearing Islamic attire." By this standard, the majority of Muslims, including my own two sons, could easily be labelled extremist. I feel some caution is needed to ensure the medium does not *mangle* the message!

Upon returning to Toronto, I encountered my own pluralistic experience. I am teaching an eight-part series on "Understanding Islam" to a group called Learning Unlimited, which is comprised of 200 educated Canadians, mostly Christian and some secular. This week, the presentation was on spirituality in Islam and sharing the stage with me was a Sufi who is a holocaust survivor from Hungary. This man of Jewish heritage led the entire audience in *zikr* of Allah and His Prophet, explained the concept of Sufism better than I could ever have done, read poetry by Rumi and Rabia al Basri, and submitted to questions till he was exhausted. It was incredible to see this crowd, some who had never said the word *Allah* in their lives, chanting the *kalima*, not once but repeatedly. Later, some people came to me and said this was the first time they were spiritually touched and requested the words to be written down for them.

So, my faith reinforced, my energies recharged and my spirit rejuvenated over Ramadan and Eid, I wish to share my enlightenment with you:

"*If it's not moderate, progressive, enlightening, delightful or tolerant - then it's not Islam.*"

PEACE

An arrow from the war
has struck the dove of peace
in its breast,
drops of blood that splatter
all over the earth
as it is laid to rest
aren't black or white,
nor Arab nor Jew,
they are red
like the blood from me and you
the world had been shattered
and loyalties put to test
it was always said that East is East
and West is West
and so they will remain
enemies at best

GLOSSARY

Adl	...Justice
Allah	...God
Ayat	...Parables
Bhangra	...Punjabi disco
Eid	...The feast after the fast
Fatwa	...Non-binding religious decree
Gurdwara	...Place of worship for Sikhs
Hijab	...Female Head covering
Kalima	...Testimony of faith: "There is no God but God and Mohammad is His Messenger"
Kufi	...Male head covering
Imam	...Leader
Khutbah	...Sermon
Ijtehad	...Independent, individual thought
Ijma	...Community consensus
Munafiq	...Hypocrite
Qur'an	...The Muslim Holy Book
Ramadhan	...Month of fasting
Shahadah	...Testimony of Faith
Shaitan	...Devil
Sunnah	...Practice of the Prophet
Sunni	...A Muslim sect in the majority
Shia	...A Muslim sect in the minority
Surah	...Verse
Ulema	...Religious scholars
Zikr	...Remembrance

REFERENCES

Abdul Rauf, Feisal: What's Right with Islam: A New Vision for Muslims and the West. Harper San Francisco

Abou el Fadl, Khaled: Speaking in God's Name: Islamic Law, Authority and Women. Oneworld Publications (Oxford)

Armstrong, Karen. History of God: The 4000-Year Quest of Judaism, Christianity, and Islam. Alfred a Knopf Inc.

Chittick, William: Sufi Path of Love: Spiritual Teachings of Rumi. State University of New York Press

Feiler, Bruce: Abraham, A Journey to the Heart of Three Faiths. HarperCollins

Hassan, Riffat: Women's Rights and Islam: from ICPD to Beijing. NISA Publications

Lang, Jeffrey: Losing my Religion: A Call for Help. Amana Publications

Mernissi, Fatima: Beyond the Veil: Male-Female Dynamics in a Modern Muslim Society. Indiana University Press

Mir-Hosseini, Ziba: Islam and Gender: The Religious Debate in Contemporary Iran. Princeton University Press

Ramadan, Tariq: Western Muslims and the Future of Islam. Oxford University Press

Sachedina, Abdulaziz: Islamic Roots of Democratic Pluralism. Oxford University Press

Safi, Omid: Progressive Muslims: On Justice, Gender, and Pluralism. Oneworld Publications

Shariati, Ali & Bakhtiar, Laleh: Shariati on Shariati and the Muslim Woman. Kazi Publications

Soroush, Abdolkarim: Reason, Freedom, and Democracy in Islam. Oxford University Press

Schwartz, Stephen: The Two Faces of Islam. Anchor

Tucker, Judith: In the House of the Law: Gender and Islamic Law in Ottoman Syria and Palestine. University of California Press

Wadud, Amina: Qur'an and Woman. Oxford University Press